OLD SURREY REMEMBERED

Nicolette Heaton-Harris

Published by Sigma Leisure – an imprint of
Sigma Press, 1 South Oak Lane, Wilmslow, Cheshire SK9 6AR, England.

British Library Cataloguing in Publication Data
A CIP record for this book is available from the British Library.

ISBN: 1-85058-645-4

Typesetting and Design by: Sigma Press, Wilmslow, Cheshire.

Printed by: MFP Design & Print

Cover illustration: Dustmen of Guildford Borough Council. Photograph taken in Bedford Road, circa 1906. Printed with permission from Surrey Records.

Preface

This book of history is compiled entirely from the memories of the citizens of old Surrey. This is an oral history, filled with simple facts and knowledge. However, as most of us appreciate, memories are subjective. Two people witnessing a place or event will remember it totally differently many years later. Therefore, I have made every effort to corroborate the information, but am surely aware that some misinformation may have slipped through the net of research. For this I apologise and hope that I may be forgiven.

I hope these accounts make readers aware of the rich history available at their fingertips. They have only to look to an older relative to hear a tale or two of the past, and this book has been created so that many such stories are not lost forever. You don't have to be a king or a queen for your history to be important enough to be recorded. Everyone makes their own unique contribution to history, and we are all rich sources waiting to be mined for our information.

Many different lifestyles have been described within these pages, and all the contributors have more stories to tell than I've managed to write down here. Despite the passage of time and enormous social changes, there is something within these accounts to strike a chord with us all. Children played, enjoyed their schooling and looked forward with trepidation to their first day in a job. Births, marriages and deaths were then, as now, the landmarks within a life. All of us can relate to these aspects of these tales, whether we lived in Old Surrey or not.

Pounds, shillings and pence

For those unfamiliar with pre-decimalization coinage it may be helpful to note that twelve old pence (d) equalled one shilling (s), and that there were twenty shillings in a pound (£). Only the pound is still with us! Amounts comprised of both shillings and pence were written with a oblique separator, so "3/4" meant "three shillings and fourpence". Sixpence (6d) is equivalent to 2½p, and a shilling to 5p.

Notes about Names

Not everybody wished to have their identities revealed. In these cases, I have referred to them by first names only. In those cases where not even first names were to be revealed, I have enclosed the name in quotation marks.

Acknowledgements

Unfortunately, I am unable to name everyone who has helped with this project but I am grateful to you all. My greatest thanks must go to those who contributed their reminiscences. Without you, there would have been no book. My special thanks also go to Eddie Gardner and his wife for sending me some lovely letters and photographs.

Thanks to Surrey Records and Local Studies Library, J. Mutimer, Surrey Comet, Esher Advertiser, Kingston Informer, J. Elwin, Walton Comrades Club, The Royal British Legion and Arbrook House. I am indebted to Christine and Ron Cox for their continuous feed of corroborating information, and to all the registered homes that allowed me to enter their doors and interview their residents!

To anyone I may not have mentioned, I apologise. Everyone was kind and helpful towards me whilst I worked on this project. My thanks go to my family and to my husband, Nicholas – I could not have done this without your support. Thank you everyone.

Nicolette Heaton-Harris

Contents

1

A Glimpse into Surrey's Past

Walter, a local historian, born in Wallington in 1907, provided much information for the transport chapter that follows, but he also told me of other aspects of Surrey's history.

'Brewing was a thriving industry in Surrey. Beer had been a staple drink for many years, and there seemed no good reason for it to stop being so. Most of the larger towns such as Leatherhead and Guildford had two or more main breweries. In 1900, there were fifty breweries in Surrey alone! Most of them have now disappeared.'

I asked Walter about famous characters from Surrey history. 'Well, I'm not too sure if you'd call him famous, but one Surrey man did have a village named after him. He was, by all accounts, a very kindly man, who had great concern for the well-being of others. His name was William Whiteley, Sir William Whiteley. He founded the Whiteley stores in London. He died the year I was born, I think, and apparently left a million or so pounds in his will for a village to be built between Cobham and Walton-on-Thames, solely for old people. They did build it, and there's a monument to Sir William there too. Quite a quaint place I've been told. I did go there once, passing through on one of my many rambles, but it's so long ago I can't remember too many details about the place. After the First World War, many estates were built along the new roads. I guess that's why Surrey seems more urban today than it used to. It had always been such a rural county, filled with fields worked by the many farmers who grew wheat and oats, or supplied London with its milk. After the Second World War, many more houses had to be built to replace all the ones bombed during the fighting. Many people needed rehousing, so they started to build tower blocks. Dreadful things that ruin the skyline and spoil the view of the wonderful horizon.'

Next on my list of questions was recreation. I asked Walter if he

A 1918 Surrey wedding: the great-grandparents of the husband of Nicolette Heaton-Harris.

knew anything of the history of the traditional sports that are played today. 'That's easy. The oldest sport is hunting. Deer was popular with royalty. Venison was their chief dish, as many people know. Then foxes and badgers were hunted, the foxes over many miles, chased by riders with packs of yelping hounds. Go into any stately house open to the public and you'll see up on the walls, the portraits of kings, queens, dukes and earls, all with their favourite hunting dog. Or perhaps there will be a painted scene of an actual hunt. Medieval royalty enjoyed hunting with falcons and hawks, but in my time a lot of hunting was done with a gun.

'Dog racing was popular, but the horse racing at Epsom became the most fashionable pastime. Then there was fishing upon the many waterways of Surrey. The water supply was clean and free of pollutants. There was also rowing, cycling and car racing at Brooklands, where the first RAC Grand Prix was held in 1926. Of course, men enjoyed boxing even if the womenfolk didn't. Bare fist fighting went on, but it was quite rare.

'Football was, and still is, popular in Surrey. There's good football history in Dorking, you know. In the nineteenth century it was usual for the whole town to take part in a game on Shrove Tuesday. The ball was taken through town to a fixed point held and defended by the other side. The game always lasted until sundown and the rules were "anything goes". You could pick the ball up with your hands, kick the other side, bite them or beat them with a stick. Luckily for the people of Dorking, the police stopped the tradition of the game and the ensuing Ash Wednesday injuries. They played this type of football in Kingston market place too. I once heard that sometimes the players would jump in the Thames and swim up river with the ball! Obviously though, this sort of physical violence stopped and the more traditional game as we know it was taught in the local schools.

'In Surrey, for those that still desired the physical contact, rugby was played. Those that required a more pleasant and less bloody pastime opted for golf. The Surrey heaths and land are ideal for courses, and there are still many here today. Women enjoyed croquet, and then the more physically demanding game of tennis, especially when they were allowed to play at Wimbledon. However, if I had to name a single pastime or sport that Surrey is most famed for, it would have to be cricket. There's a green at Giggs Hill in the Dittons where village cricket has been played for decades. Kennington Oval was the headquarters of cricket in Surrey. It had once been a market garden. The last test match is always played at the Oval. It belongs to the Duchy of Cornwall, and that is why the Surrey badge is the Prince of Wales's feathers. There have been a few famous cricket players from Surrey: Laker, Lock and the Bedser twins. P.G.H. Fender, a captain, made a century in thirty-five minutes. There are many cricket clubs in Surrey, including women's cricket clubs. You take a drive out in Surrey on any weekend during the season and you'll find village cricket being played all over the county.'

2

From Trams and Trolley Buses to Concorde

We met Walter, with his knowledge of local history, in the previous chapter. In this chapter, he provides us with a short history of the early days of transport in Surrey.

'The London to Croydon railway was opened in 1839. It was soon extended to continue from Croydon to Epsom via Dorking and Godalming then to Portsmouth. Railway was the fashionable traffic, killing off the popularity of horses and carts. There were many lines built connecting the little towns in the county, and they were all overused. By the time the First World War began in 1914, the railways were in need of extensive repair and, of course, cars were beginning to become quite popular. The Surrey lines became part of the Southern Railway at the Government's order, and the lines were electrified. Of course, it wasn't until 1896, that you could drive a car without having a gentleman waving a red flag walking in front of you. People enjoyed walking or cycling to work. Women would think nothing of walking the few miles to another town to fetch items they couldn't get at their own village stores.

'It wasn't until after the First World War that a bus network sprang up. Dorking, Leatherhead and, I think, Guildford became the epicentres of these networks. Not many people could afford motor cars, they were for the privileged few, but those that did afford them were not content with the state of roads that up until then had been used almost exclusively by horses. They were too narrow, the road surface was too stony and covered in sandy dust. The Ministry of Transport took control of the main roads, those being the A3, the A23 and the A30, the old mail coach roads. As cars became more popular and

A Dennis truck *(Surrey Records)*, circa 1920s

available to the average man, the first traffic jams were reported, and that's how Kingston got its bypass in 1925.

'In Guildford in 1904, the Dennis factory was opened, repairing bicycles, building motor lorries, cars and charabancs. A housing estate was named after them: Dennisville. The factory's still going today. Look at any fire engine or dustman's lorry and you can bet it's a Dennis.

'In 1915, the firm of Vickers took over an automobile works at Weybridge. They built the Vimy bomber and other planes for the Royal Air Force. Wellington bombers were also made there. An old Wellington pulled from a Scottish loch is currently being slowly restored at the old Brooklands racetrack. The Vickers firm grew rapidly, and gave us famous names such as Viscount, VC10 and Valiant bombers. Apparently, for a time, they even built guided missiles there. At Kingston, you could find another great name in flying history: The Sopwith Aviation Company. Then there was the Hawker-Siddeley company that built the Hurricane and the Hawker-Hunter. It's a great pleasure to live in a county that produced some of the fine fighting machines that helped us to win the two world wars.

'When the First World War broke out, the aircraft industry was given a boost. Croydon became the London terminus. The town grew in its importance, with daily and weekly services to other countries. Croydon declined after the Second World War, when London Airport was built. Gatwick had opened in 1930 as an aerodrome and that handled much of the air traffic.

From the late twenties to the early thirties, Mr Stanley R. Smith lived at Thornton Heath. He kindly shared his knowledge of travel at that time. The tram service then running from the Elephant and Castle in London, through Kennington, Brixton, Streatham and Norbury to the pond at Thornton Heath was extremely regular. At Thornton Heath the trams used to turn to Purley and Croydon. There were penny fares or you could buy an all-day ticket for a shilling. This gave unlimited travel on the tramlines. The trams ran on lines called "setts", which were extremely dangerous to the horse-drawn traffic of carriages and carts, then still very popular. Cyclists and riders of motorbikes had to watch their routes, too. If it rained, there was an extra hazard. Trolley buses eventually replaced the trams. Running on pneumatic tyres, they were quieter, more comfortable and quicker.

In those days, Croydon Aerodrome was the official airport for London, and Mr Smith recalls with fondness the old Imperial Airways H-Class Handley Page Biplanes, with four huge engines that could fly all the way to Paris. The windows were wide and larger than those in aeroplanes today, and the seats were made by Lloyd Loom. Stanley first flew at Croydon in a First World War Avro Biplane, yet when he celebrated his ninetieth birthday, he flew in Concorde. A huge contrast in style and manufacture.

He used to do a lot of walking, strolling from East Croydon, through Riddlesdown and Coulsdon to Reigate and being in open country and fields all the way. The thirties changed the countryside greatly, he recalls, with the increase in the use of cars and motorbikes. New roads were built to cope with the growing traffic, and something called ribbon development became the order of the day. The Kingston bypass began at the Robin Hood Gate of Richmond Park then went through New Malden and Tolworth to the Portsmouth Road of Hinchley Wood. This was eventually extended, as Hampton Court Way, through to the Hampton Court Bridge. This bridge was officially opened by the then Prince of Wales, Edward VIII. Interestingly, the Surrey and Middlesex boundaries were in the centre of the bridge, and it was lit on the Middlesex side by gas and on the Surrey side by electricity.

During all this development, the papers were full of advertisements informing the populace of Surrey of all the houses and estates being built. Prices ranged from £399 to £950. These were usually all freehold, with no legal fees and no road charges. The houses priced at £399 were built in The Berrylands at Surbiton, a place that had been open fields, and at West Molesey. They still stand today, but are much more expensive!

After Mr Smith married, he and his wife bought a house in Esher Road, East Molesey, near Imber Court, on an estate that had been developed by a man named Bill Hallt. The three-bedroomed, detached house with garage cost them the princely sum of £800. Then, Esher Road was a small country lane bordered by a thick, rambling hedgerow. Beyond was a cornfield that extended all the way to Hampton Court. Subsequently, this area has been developed.

In 1929, Eddie Gardner's family moved from a flat in Barnes, near Hammersmith, to a brand new house in Tolworth, arriving by tram. When they moved, Eddie was already part of a large family with five children. Over the next six years, three more children were born. His father was a keen motorist and cyclist, instilling his love for his hobby into his children. Each child was given a bicycle on which to explore the local area. For Eddie, this meant wonderful trips to Oxshott, Leatherhead and Box Hill. His father worked as a driver for the News Chronicle and Star. (These were national and evening newspapers.) So, the Gardners were one of the few families around to own a car from the twenties onwards.

Eddie's eldest brother, after learning to drive, used to take his younger siblings out for rides at weekends, exploring Surrey. Eddie's early recollections of Tolworth were of the wide, open fields, especially the area now occupied by Tolworth Broadway. He remembers

1938 Austin 7 in Kingsmead Avenue, Tolworth *(Eddie Gardner)*

350cc BSA motorbike *(Eddie Gardner)*

sliding down a haystack not far from the present site of Tolworth Station. Of course, the railway had not been built all the way to Tolworth, and the A3 went only as far as Hook and Surbiton. There was an incredible amount of open farmland that had not yet been built upon.

The Ace of Spades at Hook was a roadhouse with facilities for petrol. There was also a swimming pool and a restaurant, and people would drive all the way from London to have a night out there. Today, the Ace of Spades is just a very busy roundabout. When motoring in the 1930s, it was no problem to pull off the road at any point in your journey, go into a field and have a picnic. If driving out on a Sunday, everybody made sure they had plenty of fuel, for there were not many petrol stations open on the Sabbath.

Eddie's eldest sister, Marion, joined the Land Army and worked on several farms in Surrey, one of those being the farm near the Drift Bridge Hotel, situated near Epsom. Whilst still a schoolboy, Eddie recalls freewheeling on his bike down the many hills of Oxshott. 'They seemed huge at the time, but now they look quite small. It was considered a very daring thing to do!' Cars in the 1930s were less efficient and less reliable than those of today, but Eddie prefers the earlier days because of the greater freedom of the road. Traffic was not heavy.

Today, the huge Tolworth Tower stands in the town, dominating the skyline for miles around. Below that is a busy roundabout above the A3. That roundabout used to be a huge pond, filled with ducks, swans and geese. The pond was surrounded by open fields, trees and fruit bushes. The children of the time used to spend many free hours eating freshly picked fruit from the bushes whilst feeding the birds as they glided upon the water's cool surface. 'Such is the face of modernisation.'

3

Kingston-upon-Thames

I first met June Pearce in 1997. A grand old lady of eighty-eight, she was small, stocky and very forthcoming. She answered my request for recollections of her life with some fervour. Later in this chapter an equally-spritely 85-year-old adds her contribution.

'Years ago, towards the end of the First World War, we used to have these open-top trams, with a metal arm above to connect them to the cabling, and rails upon the roads. Every time the tram went over a junction, it was very noisy and it used to judder and shake you about! You could almost believe you were having your bones shaken out of your body. The driver couldn't turn the tram around, so they used to build them with a wheel at each end. They used to go from Thames Ditton to Kingston Hill, and they also had one from Thames Ditton going to Richmond Park Gates. As I mentioned before, they couldn't turn around, even when they went right up to the top of that hill where the hotel is now, on Oldham Road. If it rained and you were on the top of the trolley bus, as we called them, they had a kind of apron or mackintosh that went over your laps. So your hair got wet, but not your skirt. Then you had your ordinary trolley bus with a conductor. Every now and again along his route, the conductor used to get out and put a ticket in a machine that stood in the road. The machine was like a time clock and it used to punch a little time on his ticket to say when the tram had arrived. So they often dilly-dallied if they were too early.

'Every Monday morning we had a cattle market in the square just in front of Woolworth's. Nothing else but cattle, sheep, pigs and horses. There was a font there, I think it's still there today, with a trough below for all the animals to drink from if it was a hot day. They used to auction off all the animals and clip the pigs' ears. They squealed so much! It was terrible to hear! Whatever was left over

The Cattle Market *(Surrey Records)*, circa 1908

went to the slaughterhouses. There was a slaughterhouse at Cambridge Hills, but there's a EuroDollar car hire place there now. I think they sold the meat to the farmers and local butchers. My nephew, Alfie, was an animal lover, and during the dinnertime on a Monday he'd go down to market and help the farmers. He got into heaps of trouble at school because he wouldn't go back in the afternoon. He'd follow the farmers all the way back to Tolworth to help herd the cows. The market went on for years – after Monday it became a fruit and vegetable market. Then it left the square and went to Wheatfields. But that's a car park now.

'Bennetts', the fishmongers, were at the market and had a huge tank outside filled with river eels. People used to love jellied eels then. But they'd never kill the eels until you asked for some, just so you'd know they were fresh. Then there was Folletts', the butchers. It was a family business. I can remember Christmas time, it was gorgeous there. They had a "Cheap Day" on Thursdays, and my mum used to walk all the way from Chertsey to buy meat. In the window they had lovely displays of rabbit, chicken and ducks. But mainly mum used to buy pease pudding and faggots, all wrapped up in paper. Pease pudding, if you're wondering, was split peas, boiled down. More like your mushy peas of today. Mum used to ask me and Gladys what we fancied for our tea and we always asked her to go to Bennetts' the fishmongers because of the crabs' legs. For sixpence, you could get a load of crabs' legs that were left over after they boiled the crab. The legs used to fall off in the hot water, you see. They were a real luxury back then. Gladys used to crack the legs with pliers and I'd scoop out the meat. It was the sweetest thing you could ever taste! Much better than the meat in the main crab body. Also at the market was a place called Sausage and Mash. We never had anything from there, but we wanted to. It looked and smelt divine. We used to go and peer through the window at the vats of floating onions and laid out sausages.'

I then asked June to tell me about her childhood. She began with her family. 'There were seven of us, but one of my sisters was killed when she came out of church. She'd seen a piece of silver paper in the road and bent to pick it up. A car came along and hit her. Killed her outright. She was only eight years old. We never went to that church again. There was a place we used to pass on the way home called Asylum Road, where all the Italians lived. Their doors opened directly on to the pavement, they didn't have any gardens. I remember they kept donkeys down there, and a man used to make and sell windmills. There was a goldfish seller and the "Cat Man". He used to sell cat food – meat stuck on a skewer. As he came riding down our street, ringing the bell on his bike, all the cats used to follow him, tails in the air, meowing. It was like the Pied Piper of Hamelin. On Sundays, the Italians used to come around selling winkles. A bit of vinegar, salt or pepper and they were lovely. We always had some if we could afford it.

'My Dad died when I was only three. That meant that they were going to put me in a home. Fortunately, my elder sister and her husband moved in, so I stayed. Unfortunately, they had six kids of their own and it was only a three-bedroom house! We were ever so cramped. The toilet was at the bottom of the garden: a little, wooden shack with a circular hole in the door. It was scrubbed clean every day. There was no loo paper so we used newspaper, tiny squares attached to a piece of string. Sometimes, we wouldn't notice that there wasn't any paper in there and we'd shout for mum. She always came running

Swimmers photographed at Castle Street Baths *(Surrey Records)*, 1920s

with paper for us that she'd push through the little window. We didn't have a bathroom, just a galvanised bath, a bungalow bath they called it, that we used to put in front of the open grate in the living room. I always tried to get the first bath so I'd get the clean water! When we were all done, we'd hang it on the wall outside.

'We used to get swimming lessons at the local baths. They had tiny cubicles for us to get changed in and hang our clothes. They were more like cupboards. In the pool there was a thin plank of wood that you had to get on to show the teacher that you could do the swimming stroke. If you were judged proficient, you were allowed into the water. Our teacher used to have this long pole with a hook at the end and if we got into difficulty, she'd hook our costumes and lift us out! But that was a very long time ago and I was very young. Opposite the swimming baths was a tiny bread shop where you could get a little piece of unbuttered bread for a ha'penny. We always went there.

'Our job at the weekend, Saturday, I think, was to fetch the coke. We never had coal. Every Saturday morning, we'd be off with our barrow. Now, small pieces were called shingles, the larger pieces, coke, and we always thought we were getting more if we asked for shingles. Sometimes they were red hot and smoking and we thought our little, wooden barrow would go up in flames. But it never did. To get to the coke factory, we had to go down this passage which was so narrow at one end, the wheel hubs would catch. Usually, though, we'd get someone to lift the barrow over the posts for us and we'd carry on our merry way. Our other jobs were to clean the brass strips that held down the lino on our stairs – we didn't have carpets then – and to wash shoes and clothes in a copper tub in the kitchen.

'During the first war, we used to sprinkle disinfectant around the beds in the air raid shelter to keep it smelling nice. We were sometimes down there for weeks! We took it in turns to go up and out to get an urn of tea in the mornings. Kingston got damaged quite a bit, especially Park Road. Quite a few people were killed there.

'As we got older, my sisters and I used to go to this shop near Kingston Bridge. They had beautiful cakes in the window. Adjoining the bridge was a place where they had dances. We used to watch and think, "When we get older ... !" You could watch all the loving couples dancing and swaying, the women wore beautiful dresses. Next door to Milletts' was a very high-class restaurant – they do say that there's a preservation order on it now. They held dances there, too. The women seemed so gorgeous and so rich! We were just poor and envious! Boots was in Thames Street, and out the back they had a tanning yard for the shoes. It smelt terrible! I had to hold my nose to pass.

People on our street, Linden Crescent, used to like to back the horses, and thought nothing of walking all the way to Epsom for Derby Day. We used to have a lovely day and we'd take a little picnic. We'd cut through Marsh Lane then Tolworth, straight to Epsom. We'd also walk to Hampton Court Palace if they had a fair. Pack a couple of sandwiches, dress our best and have a wonderful day! By the time we got back our feet were so dirty, Mum was disgusted!

'I can also recall that there was a place called St Peter's Passage, which you went through to come out in Cambridge Road. Here was St Peter's School. It was a very old building. During the war, they'd open a door, sort of like a serving hatch, and sell soup to anyone who needed it. It was ever so nice. Another place was the East Surrey Barracks. They had a lot of meat there and used to give away the dripping. My sister Gladys and I used to get this huge basin and have it filled. Then we'd take it home and have bread and dripping for tea. There was also a place called Steadfast, down by the river. Maud and Sheila used to go there for the dances, but if it was hot they'd never go in the dance hall, They would just sit next to the river with their feet in the water. Maud lost her shoe once!

'My sister, Gladys, she used to like cycling. She went everywhere on her bike. She was once carrying flowers for a friend in hospital when her bike wheel got caught in the tram rails and she went flying over the handlebars! Another time, she forgot her bike and left it outside Woolies. When she went back for it, it was still there and it wasn't even locked. Try that today.

'When I began work it was at the VP – Vinery Products. It was on Villiers Road and they made wine. Towards the end of my twenty-nine years there, I became a supervisor of seventeen girls. I worked there during the Second World War. The factory was set out in parallel lines for production. A couple of girls along each line. We had a labeller and filler, and huge vats of wine up above our heads. They did all sorts there: sherry, red and white. The bottles came out of one machine and into another, where they were filled. They then went to the corking machine – that looked like a funnel. The corks would come

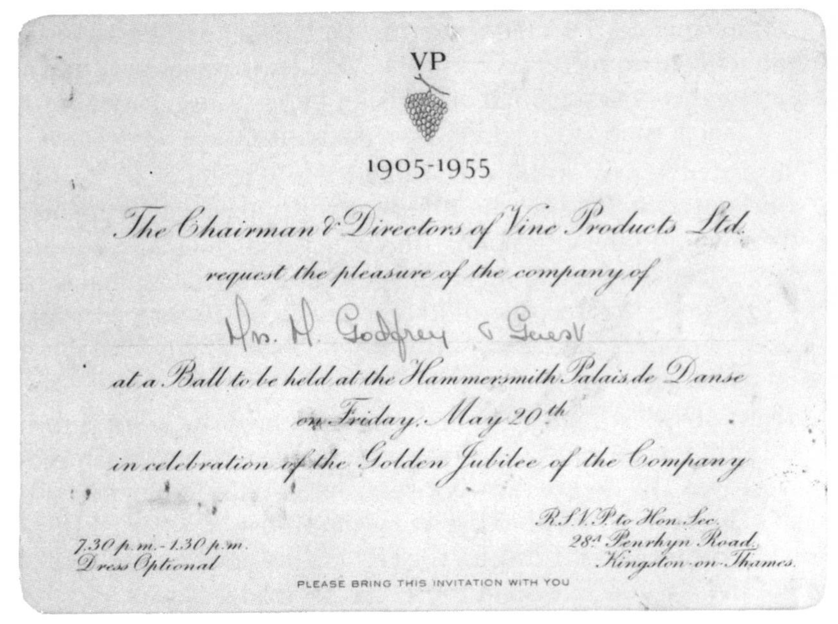

VP

1905-1955

The Chairman & Directors of Vine Products Ltd.
request the pleasure of the company of
Mrs. H. Godfrey & Guest
at a Ball to be held at the Hammersmith Palais de Danse
on Friday, May 20th
in celebration of the Golden Jubilee of the Company

7.30 p.m.-1.30 p.m.
Dress Optional

R.S.V.P. to Hon. Sec.
28a Penrhyn Road,
Kingston-on-Thames.

PLEASE BRING THIS INVITATION WITH YOU

Invitation from Vinery Products to the Hammersmith Palais

whizzing down and thump! In they'd go. Then they went to a labelling machine that one of the girls operated with a foot treadle. But if there was anything special coming through it was all done by hand.

'Once, all these tiny, ornamental bottles came through and Mr Brown told me that we had to weigh them all! Apparently, the china glass wasn't all the same thickness and the drink was an expensive spirit so the measure had to be just right! Then I can remember a huge order for a drink made up entirely of egg and brandy. I can't remember what it was called. Egg flip, or something. We worked on that order for days but we had a problem one day. We used to come into work at eight in the morning, but the laboratory people came in at nine o'clock. One day they tested it and said it was all wrong. It couldn't be sold, so the factory gave it all away! A friend and I got a barrow and loaded it up to take home. We supplied our street with it. Everyone loved it and kept asking for more! Then they began to manufacture this huge, blue glass bottle that customers were meant to keep plants in. They were ever so expensive, so not too many of those were made. At Christmas, Mr Brown came round and gave all the girls a drink of Bristol Cream for all our hard work!

'At the Vinery, I'd sometimes be asked to test a wine and give an opinion. I hated doing that because I never liked to drink. My dad had been teetotal and alcohol had never been in the house. I always used to say it tasted nice, even when it was horrible!

'Towards the end of the war, I had to do a watch. Looking after three girls in a small hut in the Vinery. If the raids came in the morning, we'd work in the afternoons, and vice versa. Some days we'd go in at five o'clock, with tea, sugar and our helmets. During that time, I had to go into Esher, too. It would take me about an hour to walk it, there were no buses then. But I didn't mind. It's probably why my legs are so bad now!'

As our interview came to its end, I asked June if she knew how her present address came to have its unusual name of Watersplash Close. 'Oh, yes. Next to here was a brewery, and running alongside it a stream. The brewery used to use horses to transport their barrels on carts. The bridge was too tiny for the carts so the horses used to splash through the stream. They had those narrow bridges quite a lot back then.'

Mrs Thomas was a tiny lady whom I met one surprisingly warm, October day. She was sitting in her lounge, reading a paper, looking very serious indeed. It was totally the wrong impression. This eighty-five-year-old lady, though totally deaf, was so full of verve and excitement that her eyes practically shone with an internal fire all of their own!

'I was born in Kingston-upon-Thames in September 1912. I grew up with two sisters and one brother. We all lived in a very small house, it was almost a cottage, really. I went to St Agatha's Roman Catholic School. A lovely place. I had my first communion there. In fact, I was baptised, confirmed, had a holy communion and then got married, all at the same church! My family had a very strong faith and connection with our church. Like a second family to us.

'I could never travel when I was younger. I used to suffer from the most horrendous travel sickness. I couldn't even go on a one-penny bus ride. I particularly remember when I was seventeen and our family was going to Bournemouth for a holiday. A two-week, bucket-and-spade affair. We got on the bus at Kingston Station, but I didn't get any further than Tolworth, which is only a mile away, if that, before I threw up everywhere! The driver had to stop the bus to clean everything up. Coming back from Bournemouth, I got on another bus and, would you believe, it was the same driver as before! When he saw me he said, "No! Don't you come on here and do the dirty again!" But I was all right coming back, strangely enough. As I got older, I found I could travel on the old steam trains. That was okay.

'When I started working, it was at a place called Daisy's. I worked in soft furnishings, making up curtains and all that. Then I moved to Bentalls', a good, family-run store. But, of course, Bentalls' is a huge shopping centre now. I used to work forty hours a week to start, but then I got my hours cut down.

'By 1937, I wasn't working, and I was married that year. My husband worked in army munitions. He was doing long hours when war broke out. After seven years of marriage, I had a baby girl. But when she was born, I didn't see her for three days. It was scary. The nurses used to tell me she was thriving, but I needed to see for myself. So, one day, a big Scottish nurse called Sister McDonald brought this ball of wriggling pink swaddling to me and I saw my baby for the first time.'

I asked Mrs Thomas if any one memory stood out particularly vividly. For her two choices she recalled her schooldays. 'When I was in my last year at infants' school, I was presented with the New Testament by the mayoress of Kingston, Mrs Finney. There was a boy of my age who was also presented with one. I will always remember him. He lived in Norbiton, the other side of Kingston, and his name was Bernard Torney. But I have to say, my other fondest memory is through my sport. For play and recreation, I used to play a lot of netball, and I made it on to the school team. I was also heavily into running. In my last year at school, in 1926, I made it into the 100-yard dash final. The last year of school, the last race. It was a big moment. I'd made it through the qualifying heats and there I was. Only I lost. I'd really wanted that winning pink ribbon. I'm quite short and all the other girls were taller than me. I can recall my mother, who was watching me that day, coming over to me and commiserating. She said, "Fancy putting all those big girls in the final with a little one like you!" I said to her, "We're all the same age, mum. Their legs are just longer than mine!"

4

The Girls of Bonner Hill School

Here are the stories of four girls who all went to Bonner Hill School. They went on to very different lives and careers, but in this chapter they all share memories of their schooldays.

Miss G. was born 28 May 1909 in Linden Crescent, Norbiton. She lived in the house for a full eighty years. The house itself was tiny. No bathroom, no toilet. If a member of her family wanted a bath, they had to wait – Monday was bath day. They all took it in turns to climb into the portable tin bath that they placed before the fire in the living room. They had a rota to decide who was lucky enough to get in first, to get the hottest and cleanest water. Afterwards, the bath was dried and placed outside under a cover to prevent insects and wildlife taking refuge inside it.

At the age of five Miss G. went to Bonner Hill School, which she attended until she was fourteen. She had a uniform of green tunic, white blouse, yellow and green striped tie and green underwear. They were allowed a single pocket for the placement of a handkerchief. First thing in the morning the register was called, then the first lesson of the day was reading scripture. Her school holidays were spent playing in Richmond Park. 'There's one entrance in Mills Street and another in Portland Drive. We felt lovely and safe there. All that open space. The tall trees rustling in the wind as the deer stood in their shadows and munched the grass.'

When she left school, she went to work for Kelly's Directories. By then, it was 1923. The firm of Kelly's eventually moved to Andover, but her mother would not let her go with the company. For three or more years she stayed at home, helping her mother. She then got herself another job at James Burns, an Esher bookbinding company, where she stayed for thirteen years. By that time war had begun. 'The air raids were so bad. So terrifying, never quite knowing if you'd be leaving the shelter when others couldn't. Sometimes, we'd stay in them all day, just in case. At the end of the working day a small coach used to pick us up and drop us off on Ashdown Road, Kingston. I can remember many a time walking into the garden and hearing my mum shout that they were in the shelter – and so was my dinner! I'd eat, then my sister and I stupidly used to sneak out from the shelter when we were bored and go back inside our house. We thought we'd still be safe sleeping under the stairs. We were lucky. Very lucky.'

All their food was rationed, even the basic items such as margarine, eggs and, especially, meat, which was to become very rare. Milk was given out in a powdered form. Miss G went to work for a company in Villiers Road and was put on a fire watch for one night a week. Three Greek brothers ran the firm and it was a happy place to work. When she turned sixty-one, she retired. 'I'd never married, never was interested in that. All my life I'd worked and looked after my mother, who died aged seventy-one. My dad, who worked for a building company, had died when he was forty-seven, so my sister and I had looked out for one another. It was what you did. It was family. We had good friends, but a horrible family doctor. His services were free, we never paid, but he was nasty to poor people. Really vindictive.'

Kingston for Miss G. and her family was a very pleasant place to live. 'The shopping areas were wonderful in particular. People came from all around to shop and there were many different races of people, just like today. The market was excellent. Fruit and vegetable stalls, cakes and sweets, fresh meats. If you went late on Saturday you could get really cheap meat from Webb's the butchers. He was only going to throw it out if he didn't sell it! At Bennetts', the fish shop, you could buy a mixture of fish pieces at the end of the day. It certainly paid to know when the cheap food was on offer if you didn't have much money. We went to Moor's, the Sausage King, if we had a bit of spare cash, just for a treat. But that was never very often. In Kingston, you had to know where free food was given out to those in need. Some places asked for a small donation, and you'd gladly give if you could. My sister and I often went out with a large basin and came back with it filled to the brim with jams, or pickles, or dripping. On Sundays you could hear from your door the Salvation Army playing their music on the bandstand, and singing so loudly! Afterwards, in the afternoon, you'd hear the squeaking of an old bike and a bell being rung as a man, whose name I never knew, used to come around and sharpen knives and scissors. All of that's gone now. It's a shame that time moves on.'

Mrs G. Preddy was born at 52 Vincent Road, Norbiton. Like most others, her family's house was small, with no amenities. She has fond memories of her short time at Bonner Hill School and of its headmistress, Miss Wag, and two teachers, Miss Patel and Miss Darling. Netball was her favourite activity and each year she participated in the school's sports day. Unfortunately, she had to leave when she was fourteen, and she went to work for H.D. Symons Parkworks on Kingston Hill. The staff were kind and polite, and everyone pulled together to help others when war began. The conditions were very frightening. Those same work mates and friends helped to celebrate her marriage at her local registry office. She recalls everyone being so happy when the war ended, but so sad at all the unnecessary loss of life.

There were no supermarkets for Mrs Preddy, just small traders trying to eke out their living. There was a Sainsbury's, but it was a tiny store then. There was no health service available until it was introduced by Bevan in the fifties. At that time things began to improve.

Dolly Beard was born in 1921 at 60 Vincent Road, Norbiton. The toilet for the house was outside, at the back of their extremely long garden. Not the most convenient of places when it was the of winter and you had a stomach complaint! They had a gas-powered Ascot heater that gave them hot water, but they all still bathed only once a week in front of an open fire.

'My time at Bonner Hill School was wonderful! I can remember thinking it was so large compared to me. I seemed so little. We had many different lessons and I loved them all. Sports were a favourite, especially netball, but we girls were taught how to play a good game of hockey too. I could be quite mean with my hockey stick! The teachers were very good and very kind, but they knew how to be firm and wouldn't stand any messing about. They taught us how to do cooking, sewing and housework, as well as all the normal subjects such as English, arithmetic and history. When I left, at the age of fourteen, I got a job at Bentalls' as a silver service waitress. It was very demanding.

When war broke out, the atmosphere turned very grim indeed. It was hard to keep your hopes high and smile each day. You could spend most of a day in a grimy, old shelter, listening for noises and the whistling of a falling bomb, praying constantly that it fell elsewhere. One particular thing I remember now that I think was quite funny, though then it wasn't, was being caught in our family shelter one night. My father decided that a gramophone in the shelter would be ideal. We'd be able to play music and listen to that instead of listening for the bombers to fly over. So, there we were, huddled together, calming ourselves with this lovely music, when my mother said to my dad, "Harris! I hear a bomber coming. Now turn that bloody gramophone off!"

Joan Birron was born on 4 May 1925 at 42 Cambridge Road, Norbiton. She particularly enjoyed doing the three Rs and domestic science at Bonner Hill School. During school holidays, she'd take jam sandwiches and home-made lemonade to Bushy Park near Hampton Court Palace and paddle in the water. 'You had to be careful when you fed the ducks because eventually the geese and swans would glide over. They could hiss at you something terrible and a flap of their wings could easily break your arm or leg.' Further into the park, Joan enjoyed watching the deer and large rooks, crows and wild rabbits. 'People picnic there and walk their dogs. It's very calming.'

She left school in 1939, just as war began, and found a job in a sweet shop. The site is now occupied by a restaurant called Garfunkel's. An early start and a late finish at 9.00pm was her usual day, and her mother used to collect her at night because of the blackouts. Eventually, she left the sweet shop and moved to another retail job at a baker's shop in Richmond Road. In 1942, she met and married her husband. He was a Canadian serving in the forces in this country. They had a son together and a very happy marriage. Unfortunately, her husband died in 1990. Joan never used to shop around too much, preferring to use her local, all-round trader, Hawkins, which was in the main centre of Norbiton. Local policemen patrolled the streets, some with dogs. They were all well over six feet tall and each had taken a rigorous exam to enter the force. Norbiton was patrolled on foot and each officer had a whistle and truncheon. 'I knew what policemen were for, but the only occasion I ever needed them was to ask the time. We all felt very safe on the streets then and often left our houses unlocked and our doors wide open.'

Joan's particular memory is of her father during the war. 'During the air raids, my dad would take us to the shelter one by one. He'd escort us from the house to the shelter's door, watch us enter, then go back for the next. I never understood that. Why didn't we all go at once? It's strange, but there you go.'

5

A Rascal's Tale

Everybody loves a rascal, and Jimmy Mutimer is one of the most likeable. He was born in 1918, in a land fit for heroes. Those were the days when children amused themselves with spinning tops complete with whip, hoops and steering hooks and marbles. There were open-top buses, horses and carts and very little traffic. The cars that were on the open roads consisted of the Morris Oxford, the Cowley, the Clyno, the Austin and the Model T Ford. On Sunday afternoons, men, balancing trays on their heads, would walk around the streets to sell hot muffins and crumpets. A bell signalled the muffin man's arrival in the street. Funeral processions were grim but spectacular, with the carriage being pulled by strong, black horses. Of course, Jimmy did not notice too much of this, being much too young. But this is what he did remember.

'I was born at home on Warwick Grove, Surbiton Hill, which is situated on the border of Tolworth. Warwick Grove was a line of small cottages, with minuscule front and back gardens, not much bigger than the average front room of a house. The cottages have now been demolished, and in their place stands a very modern retirement home. My mother lives in that home at her own request, so it's funny that she's gone back to where she began her married life.

'There were four of us in total – myself, Bill, Ernest and Joan. Our father was a painter and decorator. We never had much money, but our parents always saw to it that we had food in our bellies. We always had enough clothes and shoes on our feet, so I suppose we were lucky. Holidays were out of the question. We were very strict Baptists and went to chapel three times every Sunday, including Sunday school. Our mother, who was very severe, had come from a well-to-do family that owned a grocery business on Surbiton Hill. They used horses and carts for deliveries. There were many rich people in Surbiton, and the grocer's was very high-class in its nature. My grandmother, a determined lady, sold the business and decided to go into property, now all demolished. The old grocer's shop still stands, only now it's called Liberty Bell and is used as a restaurant. On the tiled doorstep though, you can still see the original name "Jamison's".

'One of the earliest things I recall is when I was five years old and kneeling on a bed upstairs in our house. An exuberant brother and sister charged into the room and jumped on the bed, which in turn reacted like a trampoline. I sailed clean out of the bedroom window and crashed into a window box on the ground floor, then rolled on to the concrete. I quickly got to my feet and prepared to run before I was smacked for leaning near a window, which gives an indication of how strict my mother could be. Instead, I was cuddled and made a fuss of and was allowed to sit in my father's chair. I revelled in being the centre of attention. All the neighbours kept a watch on me as if they expected me to lapse into a coma at any second. I pretended that I had a bad headache. The seeds were sown. I loved to be the centre of everyone's attention.

'Next came school. St Mark's School in St James Road, Surbiton. A very old, crumbly, Victorian building. To get there, I had to cross the main Ewell Road and the busy Victoria Road. I had been given strict instructions from my mother to ask anyone to help me cross the roads. You're not allowed to let kiddies speak to strangers today! The first three years of school did not have an impact on me. Naughty children were smacked on the knuckles with a ruler, and at first I kept out of trouble. Going to school, I always had to pass this beautiful house in Oakhill, with a long, sweeping driveway out into the road. Whenever I passed, a dog used to come furiously snapping its way down the drive, desperately trying to eat me! I got scared rigid and subsequently tried to find another way to school to avoid the hungry canine.'

Jimmy's memories give some indication of how the area has changed. There were times when cattle were driven up the streets from Hook, about two miles away, and driven up a ramp leading off the road of Surbiton into cattle trucks. Every so often, when a bull escaped, the school gates would be locked at playtimes until the angry animal was caught. That ramp is now the entrance to Sainsbury's in

Victoria Road, and leads you round the back of the store to the main car park.

'Whenever the snow was thick on the ground, on Saturdays my father used to take me and my brother and sister all the way to Richmond Park on a tram. We used to prop our toboggan on the back. A huge thing it was – heavy and made of wood. I don't know how those tram drivers survived the winter. Exposed to all the elements, they'd stand deathly still through wind, hail, rain and snow, never seeming to make an effort to keep warm. But whenever you got to a tram stop, you'd see the drivers, eyes streaming, stamping their feet and batting their arms against their bodies until their blue skin became all pinky red again. I know of one tram driver who did that job for forty years. He died aged 101!

'Anyway, at Richmond Park we used to haul the toboggan to the top of a hill, then we'd all jump on together and push off. Screaming and whooping, we thought it all great fun, until one day we hit a bump and the toboggan flipped over. It went into the air and came crashing down on my wrist. There were no tears. I bravely basked in all my friends' attention. "What a hero!" they'd say. We went home and my wrist swelled over the next couple of weeks. My mum had wrapped a bandage around it because we couldn't afford to give anything to our doctor. One day at school, a teacher noticed my wrist and showed it to a nurse. Within the hour, my arm was in splints and diagnosed as completely broken. Again, I had a great fuss made of me at home. I hate to think of how smug I was!

'In 1926 came the General Strike. Wages were low and unemployment was rife. I saw people throwing stones at a bus driver until the police arrived. My mother dragged me away from those "beastly people." The Welsh miners eventually gave in after a few months, having achieved nothing. Those on the poverty line throughout the country were having a terrible time. I saw kids with bare feet waiting in line outside a cake shop for a penny's worth of stale cakes. I took off my shoes and bought a penny's worth one day, just to see what they were like. They were gorgeous, actually. My mother would have gone ballistic if she'd known. My last recollection of those days was when I was eight years old and had to go to the school clinic for a tooth extraction. You sat on bare, wooden forms, watching the other kids being dragged into a room, kicking and screaming. When they came back out, they'd be sobbing quietly, tears running down their cheeks as they held a side of their mouths. It wasn't until 1946 that I lost my fear of dentists.

'We then moved to Hook, now in the expanding area of Chessington, home of the "World of Adventures". I suddenly realised that there was a beautiful side to life that I'd never noticed before – Nature! I learned about seasons, the deafening sound of the dawn chorus that came from our garden, the froth of blackthorn lining the roads, and the fact that there was life and colour blossoming everywhere. The long, hot days of summer were filled with the scent of freshly mown hay, the rich, green grass was dotted with red poppies and dog daisies that we picked by the armful. Then there was Bluebell Woods, a small coppice that currently stands by the Esher bypass. In autumn, there was an abundance of pickings: apples, blackberries, mushrooms, chestnuts, cob nuts, conkers, hips and haws, corn, barley and oats. And winter was filled with freezing days in which to go tobogganing and skating on ponds. One pond we called "The Bluey". It was where the Gala factory now stands on the A3. All the different ponds around meant that we never went short of tadpoles during the spring, and I recall many a crafty dip in the buff, drying ourselves with our vests afterwards.

'Our house, 289 Hook Road, has since been demolished. It had a large kitchen, which back then was called a scullery, with a gas stove in it and a huge boiler for washing clothes. There were two reception rooms, so we had plenty of space for a change. The kitchen had one of those old ranges that blackened until it shone. My mother loved to cook in there, but hated washing the clothes and then wringing them out with the hand-operated mangle. We took in a lodger, to help with the budget.

'We had a long garden filled with fruit trees, and they made a wonderful sight in the spring with all their blossom. There was a cooking apple tree that, year in and year out, supplied a bountiful crop of fruit the size of grapefruits. We also had a Blenheim Orange tree, and even though its trunk was hollowed out halfway up, it gave out plenty of apples. At night, you'd hear the tawny owls calling from within it, and if I watched long enough, I'd see them flying in or out. Then there was a pear tree, a Cox's apple tree and a cherry tree. My father rarely pruned them and never sprayed them.

A 1920s housewife at work *(Joyce Gardner)*

'At the bottom of our garden was a school playground – a place I was destined to go. To get there, I'd nip over the fence. Next door but one was a chicken farm owned by a Mr Sims, so whenever mother wanted eggs, she could buy them still warm from the nest. Opposite the house was a small bakery owned by Lewis's, and now an estate agent's. Behind the bakery was an orchard owned by "old man Phipps". He spoke with an affliction that sounded as if he spoke through his nose. We didn't do any scrumping in his orchard, just played cowboys and Indians or tree climbing. Don Lewis, a son of the baker, was with us one day when we were up a tree and old man Phipps turned up, shouting and waving a stick. Don fell out of the tree with fright and broke his arm. We all ran off. The old man never caught up with us. If he had he would have lain about us with his stick. There would have been no repercussions for him doing so. It would have served us right for doing wrong.

'Our garden flourished, no doubt helped by the tons of horse manure we'd collect from the road. We'd use a four-wheeled box cart and get paid sixpence for a full load. We were almost surrounded by fields, and there was a sleeper track at the top of Orchard Road, a few yards from our house. At night, we could hear the clip-clop of a pony and trap taking Mr Fields back to his house. Mr Fields was a frequent visitor to the North Star, a pub a few doors away from us. The pony took him home every night with no help from the "happy" Mr Fields. In the mornings, I'd be woken by the cuckoo calling. I'd look out of my bedroom window and see the Epsom grandstand in the distance. Today, you can still see it if you stand on the same spot, but it's now Chessington Golf Course. There were two or three farms nearby and in Elm Road, a blacksmith. I'd love standing there, watching the red-hot iron hissing as the water was poured over. The smith never minded. Elm Road is now filled with nursing homes, one called Forge Cottage.

'Every year, my mother used to make us eat boiled stinging nettles because they were supposed to be filled with goodness. Every Saturday night we were given a dose of either Syrup of Figs or liquorice powder. On Sunday mornings we'd suffer terrible, griping stomach pains, usually just before we had to go to chapel, where we'd usually be found running to the back where the toilet was situated, then returning to worship the Lord with our cleansed and purged insides.

'Whenever our father took us to Sunday school, we'd walk the two miles through all weathers because he believed that the bus drivers shouldn't have to work on Sundays. After the school, we'd go into the chapel for part of the service, then troop out as a hymn was being sung. We'd always vary our route home, taking our time, so our mother never grew suspicious. After our roast dinner, we'd go back to Sunday school, then back home for tea and then back again for the evening service! We walked a minimum of twelve miles every Sunday, but we never minded. It was normal. Our dad continued to work as a decorator, usually in large houses where the work had to be perfect. He was a real craftsman and ran his own business. He and my grandfather used to push a handcart filled with ladders, paintbrushes and pots of paint. It had "Mutimer & Sons" on the sides. If they ever needed anything else, one of them would fetch it all the way from home. I felt his death, at the age of sixty-three, keenly.

'It was about this time that they built the Kingston bypass and I became appalled at the desecration of my beloved countryside. I never again got to see the fox cubs playing in the long lush grass. I began a new school in Hook. A Church of England building situated, as I said, at the bottom of our garden. My brother Bill and I didn't make a good start with the other kids. We'd spotted a bird's nest in the blackthorn and pulled away some of the branches to get a better look at it. At lunch time, a crowd of boys surrounded us, and one accused me of robbing the nest. He hit me in the face and my head shot back and hit the brick wall. When I went home, I was scared stiff of going back that afternoon. I was told to go back and face it like a man. I didn't. I avoided them at any cost. Gradually though, we began to make friends there. An aunt of mine had died and she'd owned an old bath chair. I took it to school and we all had great fun pushing each other around on it. Fun was cheap in those days. In total, I spent two years at Hook school. They allowed you to go haymaking, and once, in the bad weather, a car got stuck in the mud outside our school. We all went outside and gave it a push to set it free. We attended Hook parish church, just down the road. It had only weekday services. As a strict Baptist, I found the Church of England ceremonies strange. But it was fascinating and I loved the choir.'

In front of that church is the grave of Harry Hawker. He was the founder of the great planes that later filled our skies and helped to save the country from invasion during the war. 'Under the floor boarding in our bedroom at Hook, we found a piece of wood that had an inscription which claimed it was part of the propeller of the plane that crashed and killed Harry Hawker.

'There were two unusual things that I did at the church. One was bell-ringing. There were six bells and we were carefully instructed to pull the rope at the right time and to let go when the rope rose, otherwise we'd be pulled upwards into the belfry. The other job was to go into a cubby hole situated behind the great organ and pump away with a handle for dear life. This supplied the air to the organ and allowed it to play. The inevitable happened one day. Tired, I rested for a few seconds and suddenly the organ gave out a great wheeze. The congregation bravely went on singing.

'When I was ten, my mother decided we were to go back to school in Surbiton as she was tired of us mixing with "the ignorant country oafs". Nothing was further from the truth, however. This meant an incredibly long journey for me and my brother, so we got hold of a second-hand bike that we shared, taking it in turns. If we didn't use the bike; we'd ride the buses. The buses had barely altered from the ones used in 1914. They had open tops, with wooden seats and a canvas to pull over your legs in wet weather. If we were on the bike, however, we rode in the slipstream of the bus, our front wheel inches away from the rear of the bus. Another trick was to free wheel if a lorry or truck had a rope or chain hanging from it. We'd hold on for as far as the truck went. I was doing this on a cart one day when it stopped. A very irate driver came round and told me, in no uncertain terms, to go away. Another time, I recall, I was walking and one of Stickley's carts came by. They still used the ponies and traps. The driver offered me a lift and I happily got on, innocently sitting on the shafts just below him. I should have realised what was going to happen. In front of my startled face, a horse's tail rose and there was the sound of rushing wind. Stale oats and fresh manure enveloped me. The driver nearly fell off his seat with laughter. From then on I always rode on the edge of the shafts, my lesson learnt.

'Our local shops were on the Hook Road. There were no such things as supermarkets. Material for clothing was from Mrs Brooker, shoes and cobbling was done at Mr Agga's shop, groceries came from Oakley's and candy from Seymour's. The service was personal and friendly. Everybody knew one another's name. On a side road from our school were two sweet shops that were simply converted front rooms of the terraced houses. Unwrapped sweets lay basking in the sunny windows. In one, I recall, a cat used to sit on the sweets. If you went into the shop, a bell would ring and a little old lady would come out from the back to serve you. If you asked for a penny's worth of sweets, the cat would be shooed off them, then she'd grab a handful, weigh them and then stick them in a little piece of waste paper, twisted like a cone. They didn't have paper bags and the sweets would still be warm from the cat sitting on them. I remember that one day I saw the old lady in the back room, licking discoloured chocolates and wiping them clean with her handkerchief then putting them back in the box for sale. It fair turned my stomach and I never bought chocolate from there again.

'Now I began to get into more serious trouble at school. Misdemeanours usually meant the cane, and I had a taste of it many a time. Twice I played truant and got discovered. My mother made me sit and practise my piano until my father got home. He didn't give me a good hiding, but insisted that I either own up to the headmaster and take his punishment or he'd raise his hands to me. I wanted to ward off punishment for as long as possible and said I'd own up the next day. Mr Stiling, our headmaster, was a tall man, very dapper and immaculately dressed, toting a thin, wooden cane. We all thought him quite vicious. Before class started, I went to him and told him about playing truant the day before. It took a great deal of effort to tell him without my legs collapsing beneath me in sheer terror. Mr Stiling thought, then said that he'd punish me severely if I misbehaved at all that day and the punishment would be double the norm. I hardly breathed all day! But at half past three, he called me out in front of the class and said I'd not been paying enough attention in class. I got six stripes of the cane on each hand and six on my behind. Then he said that I wasn't allowed to do any swimming for the whole term. I was a marked child until I was twelve years old and had to take an exam. I passed and was allowed to go to Surbiton County Secondary School on Wagon and Horses Hill.

'I felt lost at this school. They put me in the wrong classes and I became hopeless at maths, physics, algebra, French and chemistry. The only thing I was good at was English – and getting the cane! The school itself was a beautiful, old building with large grounds. In winter we ran around the school perimeter in shorts and a vest, and in summer we did gym every day. We also had boxing lessons, which I quite enjoyed and felt I was rather good at. I won most of my fights using my straight left, which my opponents always seemed to run into, until one year when I had an accident on my bike. I was taken to Surbiton Hospital and a doctor said to me, "Ah, yes, a dislocation." He grabbed hold of my arm and yanked it. I screamed and passed out. My elbow was broken! It was two years before my arm became normal again.

'I had my own bike by now and cycled everywhere. Once I went to

Brighton and spent the night on the seafront. I also used my bike to hunt out some excitement. This usually meant grabbing hold of the back of a fire engines as it raced to a call. I remember once, there was a fire at Gridley Miskins, a large timber yard on the banks of the Thames. It burned furiously.

'When I was sixteen, the headmaster told my parents that he thought I wouldn't pass Matriculation, the equivalent of today's "A" levels. He said it would be in my best interest to seek employment. I joined the army and stayed there until I was twenty-seven, when I was demobbed.'

6

Village People

Nowadays, many village people are newcomers – some who have moved away from suburbia, others who have bought second homes. This was not the case in the early part of this century, when many families had been in a village for generations. Read on to find what village life was like in those halcyon days.

Arthur Smith was born in 1904 in the tiny Surrey village of Outwood, situated south-east of Reigate. He was born into an unusually small family for the time, having only one other sibling – a brother, George. Arthur admits to not enjoying school. He preferred playing truant and spending his days in the woods next to the village. Inside school, he had to sit on a hard, wooden bench, reciting from the bible and doing mathematics. At the time, he thought these of no real use in the big, outside world. His teacher was strict and imposing, and not against the idea of rapping the knuckles of anyone who stepped out of line. Recreation time after school was spent playing cricket. The village's cricket pitch was situated down a tree-lined lane. Arthur fondly remembers that whenever a six was hit, the fielders would have to go into the forest to find the ball. Sometimes they were in there for an age, he recalls.

Other times, in the summer, when the nights were light, he and his friends would head west towards the river. They'd always start off fishing, but if the weather was particularly hot it usually ended in stripping down to their birthday suits and jumping in. A water fight would usually ensue. Afterwards, as darkness began to set in, they'd lie on the grass or rocks nearby to dry off before dressing, then wend their way home, picking up long sticks and having mock sword fights along the trails. If Arthur took a particular route home, he knew he'd pass the part of the wood that was covered in bluebells. Sometimes, he would pick a bunch to give to his mother, who always put them in a brown vase on the kitchen window sill.

Arthur and George's home was a small cottage with two bedrooms, one of which he and his brother shared. They had no carpets and their daily chore was to sweep out their room and make sure that their window was open to let in the fresh air. The only trouble with this, Arthur recalls, was that in autumn, leaves from the trees ended up in their bedroom, swirling about under the bed that they shared. His mother would not let them close the window, as she had a firm belief that fresh air was good for you and as long as you always had a supply of it in your room, you would never fall ill. Of course, this wasn't true. 'We always got colds in the winter. At night, we'd huddle together beneath the bed sheets for warmth, one of us sneezing and coughing, staring at that hated bedroom window that we weren't allowed to close.' Arthur and his brother wouldn't have dared to defy their mother's wish.

Weekends were spent out with their father, Thomas. They collected wood from the forests in bundles, taking it home and chopping it up into kindling for the fire. This usually took up most of Saturday morning and afternoon, depending on the time of year. The wood supply had to last all week, after all. Then in the evening, they'd go out to trap rabbits. 'Our father was an expert trapper, at least he was to us. Most Saturdays we'd come back with four or five rabbit bodies hanging from a pole that father carried. I must admit, though, that the first time our father decided we were old enough to know how to skin and gut a rabbit, I was sick. We sat outside, beneath the kitchen, near the outside toilet. I'd always thought rabbits were cute creatures that wriggled their noses when alive and tasted great after being in our mother's cooking pot. I'd had absolutely no idea on the stage in-between! George took to it better than I, and I was quite happy to let him carry on doing it.'

Towards the other side of the house, their mother grew vegetables, mostly potatoes and carrots. In those days when money was scarce and most people poor, the Smiths were quite a self-sufficient family. The farm where their father worked allowed Thomas to bring back a couple of eggs at the end of every week and a pail of milk. The only thing that Arthur recalls ever having to buy in the village was a loaf of bread every now and again, if their mother hadn't made one herself.

'Eventually though, as my brother and I got older, things got better. Father got himself a gun and we started to eat pigeon as well as rabbit. When we were old enough to start work as farm hands, the farm owner allowed us a chicken to take home each weekend, along with the usual eggs and milk. We may have been poor, but we were very rich indeed.' Then fate stepped in and introduced Arthur to his wife-to-be, Millie. After they were married, they moved to Reigate, and Arthur was startled at the difference in lifestyle. They had four children, three boys and a girl. Arthur trained as a bookbinder and was in the job until his health failed him. He retired, and after his wife passed away went to live with his daughter in Haslemere.

Patrick Baldwin was also born in 1904 but in Lingfield, which is the largest village in Surrey. His family was large: his parents, himself and five other brothers, sadly, all deceased. Patrick was the youngest child and had enjoyed being so. School had been rough and five elder brothers afforded him some protection from the knuckles of the other boys, who had a passion for boxing without the gloves. He informs me that his nickname was "Willy", but would not tell me why. His only suggestion being it would be embarrassing to tell me because I am female! Let your own imaginations run riot!

Even though bullying was rife, Patrick enjoyed his lessons at school. 'I enjoyed English especially. The language of our Queen is beautiful if spoken correctly.' His uniform was grey, with short trousers for the boys. 'White socks and polished shoes! Can you imagine young boys managing to keep their socks white and their shoes scuff-free?' Patrick recalls that girls were teased and their hair pulled to distraction in classes. If caught misbehaving, boys were given the cane and girls slapped on their hands with a ruler. 'Though I was one of the lucky few who had no association with the cane whatsoever,' which indicates that Patrick behaved. Sport held no special interest for Patrick. He simply felt that it had no excitement compared to the racecourse, where the horses galloped at high speeds. His family had gone to the races for a day and this had left their youngest son in awe. So it was that when he left school, aged fourteen, he obtained a job as a stable boy, mucking out the horses. He admits that he could have done better for himself as he felt that he had a good brain in his head, but his passion for the horses and the races overcame anything else that he felt. 'I remember a deep chestnut mare in particular. She had a blaze of white upon her face and white socks. Her temperament was amazing, such a good-natured horse. Her name was Queen something, I don't remember it correctly. I loved that horse. She was one of many I cared for during my years there, but she's the one I remember. Anyway, she had a bad fall one day when she was out training. They shot her and put her out of her misery. It was the only horse I saw shot and my last. I quit the job. I was devastated at her loss. My family couldn't understand why I'd given up such good employment with its many prospects and regular wage. But I did all right for myself. I gained employment at Puttenden Manor as a gardener. I never really saw the family of the house, just my supervisor. I know that the Napier family lived there, but I couldn't tell you if it was when I was employed there.'

Patrick never went back to the Lingfield course again, though he could frequently hear the thunderous rumble of many pounding hooves in the distance. He worked at the manor for just a couple of years before he married in his local church. 'My wife, Mary, was very religious. We went to church three times every Sunday. There was an atmosphere in church then that I don't get when I go nowadays. Everybody used to dress their best. That meant the best dresses for women with hats, and suits with ties for the men. We all knew one another's names, and it was such a friendly atmosphere. The vicar became a family friend and was often invited into our home to share a meal. We didn't have much money. I suppose we were quite poor, but we never resented sharing with others what little we had ourselves. As time went by, it became obvious that Mary and I couldn't have children. We were both quite upset there for a while. But in those days, you got on with things. You put your difficulties behind you and moved on.'

"Sally" was born in 1912 in a village called Chiddingfold, a delightful little parish. Her home was shared with another family, the Bakers, who owned the grocery store below. The Bakers were all usually working in the shop most of the day, and so the flat was their own until the shop closed at seven in the evenings.

'I was a well-behaved child. I went to school, never played truant, then came home to help mother with the flat. I swept the floors and cleaned the windows, and every couple of days, the brasses would be cleaned. We made up all the beds, and made sure that their clothes had been washed and wrung out through the mangle that we kept in the kitchen. Then mother and I would cook supper, for us and the Bakers. I admit it was a strange arrangement if I think of it now, but at the time we didn't know any different. After eating, the men would fill their pipes and smoke in one room to talk about the day, and the women would sew or we'd read aloud to each other. They were perfect evenings. Proper family time.'

"Sally" left school and began her nursing training. 'After spending my childhood looking after other people, it seemed only natural to do it as an adult.' She remembers that it was hard work, but eventually gained her nursing qualifications from her school in London. 'By the time, the Second World War had begun, I was stationed in a London hospital, but I was asked to go to Dover, to work in the hospitals there and care for the wounded coming back over from France. I saw some horrific sights. Perfectly healthy men kept going across the water and coming back with limbs missing or having lost so much blood it was impossible to save them. We all fixed them up as best we could, but it was hard. Our morale was very low, but we had to put on a smile and be cheery for the soldiers. Many of them were away from home and missing their families, just like I was.

'Thankfully, when the war ended, I returned to my safe family haven in Chiddingfold. It was back there that I caught up on all the tales of what had happened in the parish over the years. Crossglades, a large imposing house, had apparently been housing prisoners of war! But it's been pulled down now. Canadian troops had been billeted at Shillinglee Park, an eighteenth-century mansion. When the war was over they celebrated so well that they set fire to the place in their drunkenness. I felt for the fire brigade. I really did. They are another bunch of brave men who don't get paid enough for their perils. They tried their hardest to save Shillinglee, but the Canadians hampered their efforts because they were so drunk! They got the fire under control eventually and the troops sobered quickly. It was an event that made me feel weary just thinking about it. Burn wounds can be terribly painful, or fatal to some. Just the thought of all those endangered lives, especially after I'd spent all that time at Dover. It was bad enough that the soldiers' wounds had been inflicted by Germans, but these troops had done it to themselves. It was completely unnecessary. But, it was their way of celebrating the end of the conflict and I don't blame them for that. Everybody was terribly happy. The states of our lives were poor, no food, the rationing continued, but it was over. No more bombs, no more bullets. No planes roaring overhead to disturb your sleep. Unless you have lived through something like that and seen the sights that I have seen, you couldn't possibly understand what war is like.'

7

"Truth, Courtesy, Sincerity and Study"

Here are two contrasting tales, with the unusual difference being that the people featured are married to each other. They went to the same school, but were not teenage sweethearts!

Eddie first went to school at Barnes, near Hammersmith, from the ages of five to seven. It was at that tender age that he and his family moved to Tolworth. His school was Tolworth Council School, situated in Red Lion Road, and the strict but fair headmaster was named Mr Stokoe.

'It was, for me, a better school than the one I'd attended at Barnes. Here, at Tolworth, I remember that all the boys' morning milk was delivered in metal crates, on the back of a cart pulled by a horse. The bottles had a card on top with a small, ready-prepared circle to be pushed down by a straw. We all had to pay one penny for that morning break refreshment. Our school motto was "Truth, Courtesy, Sincerity and Study", and the initial letters of each word were part of the school's badge, which was worn on our uniform's cap. The initial letters also stood for Surbiton/Tolworth Council School.

'I was at the Council School from 1929 to 1933, and I was quite worried when the big day came for me to advance to the Tolworth Central School, which had opened only in 1932 in Fullers Way. The top floor of the school was for the girls and had female teachers, the ground floor was for the boys and had all male teachers. The headmaster here was still Mr Stokoe, and then there was Mr Parsons who taught English, Mr Mew – art, Mr Gay – music and gardening, Mr Speller – history, Mr Cunningham – science, Mr Robinson and Mr Houghton who taught woodwork and Mr Saunders who taught geography. The school was surprisingly modern for 1933, with two science laboratories, two woodwork rooms, and an art room. There were 360 girls and 360 boys, totally segregated. No fraternisation!

'During my first year there I gladly helped to build a fishpond at the front of the building. It's still there today, but unfortunately, is not used as such. Mr Gay was the teacher who led the project, and he also led the school drum band. In the years from 1933 to 1935, Mr Mew organised hobby exhibitions. The first year a profit of £10 was made, and in 1934 a profit of £31 – this time I was a steward. This new school had two huge playing fields and they were extremely well used. There were also allotments available for rent there, to grow flowers and vegetables. Again, Mr Gay organised and prepared the ground from its previous existence as a bracken-strewn field. Obviously there was a shortage of garden tools, and we were each asked to bring in our own spades and forks, a wheelbarrow even! I believe someone borrowed a pickaxe and I took in a small trowel. When I finally came of age to leave this school, I was fortunate enough to be able to go to a college in Essex.'

In the 1930s, Eddie and his brothers visited many parts of Surrey by car and bicycle, and one of his favourite beauty spots was by Wisley Lake. 'We easily lost each other in the vast, dense forest of pine trees.' Other favourite spots included Dorking and parts of Guildford. 'When a friend of our family bought a plot of land at Durfold Woods, near Dunsfold, in 1938, it was much used by us as a weekend retreat. We had so much fun pushing a large tank on wheels to a pump to get our water. Whilst at the pump, after playing hockey with makeshift hockey sticks that were actually tied together branches, we'd strip off our clothes to have a shower under the icy water. It hadn't been vandalism of those trees, by the way. We'd cut them down earlier to make a clearing in the wood. We ate our meals outdoors. For some reason, being outside seemed to make the food taste better no matter what it was! To clear any waste and water from our washing area, we'd created drains. It had been a lot of backbreaking digging, but it worked well and it was fun to do. Our visits to Dunsfold before the war were by Greenline coach to Guildford, then by bus to Godalming, another bus to Dunsfold, then a two-and-a-half-mile walk to Durfold Woods. Once, I clearly recall the Greenline route had been suspended, I think because of the war, and so this time we took five buses! Tolworth to Esher, Esher to Ripley, Ripley to Guilford, Guildford to Godalming and finally Godalming to Dunsfold. Any other route would have meant taking our bicycles on a train from Surbiton to Witley, and then cycling six and a half miles to our caravan. If it was a fine day, we sometimes decided to cycle all the way from home.

'When the war began, my friend's father had a building erected which purported to be an air raid shelter. The thing is, air raid shelters are not meant to have windows of glass, but it turned out that he'd been trying to get planning permission to build a bungalow and they'd not allowed it. The war gave him a good excuse to build a bungalow/shelter!'

Eddie had several favourite areas in Surrey, but Bagshot became a particular favourite after he bought a motorcycle in 1947. 'It was such a pity, though, that from the 1930s owning a car or motorbike was increasingly popular and traffic jams were frequent.'

Joyce is married to Eddie. They both went to the same Tolworth school at the same time, but they didn't meet then! Joyce also shared her memories with me.

'I lived in the Red Lion Road area of Tolworth for thirty-five years. My pre-school recollections are mostly of shopping trips into Kingston with my mother. We'd get there by tram and go to the Bentalls' store, which was then quite a small establishment, not the huge shopping centre that it is now. I can recall feeding the pigeons in the market place afterwards, and then buying our chicken feed at Thornton & Stimpson's. Our family kept hens at home, and they always produced the finest tasting eggs I ever had. When I was seven years old, I was transferred to St Matthew's school in Ewell Road. That building is now occupied by the local constabulary and I find it strange whenever I pass to see the police officers at desks in my old classroom! At that young age I was very interested in poetry reading, in fact, in all of the English subjects. There are two things that I remember quite well. I was once given a prize at eight years of age for writing an essay on "The Care of the Hair and Skin", and later, when I was ten years old, I was selected to recite a poem to the school on a fête day.

'It was after that that I finally went to the newly-built Tolworth Girls School, situated on the top floor above the boys' classrooms. Our headmistress was a Miss Helen Grant. She was a wonderful lady whom I admired, but very strict. Miss Grant introduced me into thinking of life in a totally different way. She gave us all a new outlook. She taught, produced and directed us in our Gilbert and Sullivan operas. I had always sung and she chose me to play lead soprano in *The Mikado* and *Iolanthe*. I was so proud and so very excited. We performed at the Surbiton Assembly Rooms, which still stands today, though not quite in the same manner. For sixpence a lesson we were also taught how to play the violin, which I did with gusto. We were so very pleased when our orchestra won awards at the Wimbledon Music Festivals. I also won awards there for my solo singing. This was all such a great change for me from my previous church school existence, but I do think that the teachers there were excellent. They taught me different subjects, and there were very few leavers who were not masters of the three Rs. From the girls' school, I then went on to the Kingston School of Art. Mr Reginald Brill was the principal. He came along to the girls' school and interviewed me after seeing some of my work. I was thrilled at being awarded a fine scholarship. It was all so exciting! I spent a very happy fifteen months there until my father became ill, then I had to leave to find work. There were no educational grants to assist you in those days. It has been one of my life's

1952 NAAFI production of "The Mikado" *(Eddie Gardner)*

regrets that I did not finish, but other things in my life have compensated for that.

'I found work at the United Dairies' office and stayed there for five years. It was situated in Villiers Avenue. It was extremely hard work but everyone there was very friendly and easy to get along with. The head bookkeeper arranged for me to have singing lessons with a Miss Mary Dyke. I took some exams with her. My brother and I also joined an amateur operatic society, and we both took leads in their productions of Gilbert and Sullivan. I was pleased to have quite a few engagements to sing the Messiah solos at various churches in the area, and I took part in the concert parties during the war. We performed in Leanbury Gardens some of the time. It was all part of the "Holidays at Home" plan.

'In 1941, I joined the NAAFI to work at Ruxley Towers headquarters in Claygate. I worked in the personnel department. Many of the staff had been transferred from Kennington because of the bombing and it must have been a bad move for them, having to travel each day to the wilds of Claygate! Before the European landings there was a lot of activity, but I'm sure that no-one except for the highest officials had an inkling of what was going on. We took turns doing a fire watch once a week. We slept in a tiny hut, which had a single bed and was fairly comfortable, especially when the coke fires were lit and the lights were out! Lying there, you could hear the lions roaring in Chessington Zoo, situated just a field away from us, and we often wondered what would happen should a bomb drop nearby and the carnivorous animals escape!

'I worked there for fifteen years. The Control of Engagement Order kept us there at first and we all talked of leaving, but when it all ended, very few of us actually did leave. I left to marry. If I hadn't, I'd probably still be there!

'In my childhood days, family outings were mostly local. We had picnics in Oxshott Woods and came home very dusty and dirty indeed. The soil there was black. Other picnics took place in Malden Fields, where the corn grew. Unfortunately, it has now been built on and little of it remains. Our leisure time was spent on Epsom Downs, Richmond Park and Home Park. We acquired a car when I was about fourteen. We'd drive around Surrey, to Dorking and Guildford and often to Selsey Bill, but in those days the Portsmouth road was the way to that part of the coastline and the traffic jams were endless at Esher. Traffic was bad back then. It could take a whole hour just to get through the centre of Dorking town. When the bypasses were built, we all thought them wonderful. Headley became a favourite haunt of mine, and you could walk from there to Epsom through woodlands scattered with primroses and violets in springtime. Now, some of the old pathways have been fenced off, and all that young, childlike innocence and freedom has gone. When out driving in those days it was quite accepted to just pull off the road and drive into a field to have a picnic. We'd never leave any rubbish, and after clearing up we'd be off again, leaving the field as we found it. Tidiness was a strict way of life. Back then, we had a group called the "Anti-Litter League". Badges were worn and many people belonged to the group. It was definitely a good idea. People took notice of them and obeyed the rules. I definitely doubt that it would work today.'

8

The New Malden Gang

One late November day, Patrick Denison kindly related his memories to me. Many readers will remember the years before and during the second World War. Hard times, but a period when many firm friendships were made.

'On 1 August 1938, my parents, brother and I moved into New Malden. We'd previously been living at Shoreham-by-Sea in Sussex. I believe my parents had had their honeymoon here in New Malden in the 1920s. Dad quickly found us all a house to rent in the high street, quite near the station. Our address was 3 Malden Road and we were next to The Tavern pub. Our house had four storeys, and the front was a shop called Jays the Outfitters. Renting the house cost our family £1 per week. The building had front and rear reception rooms, a kitchen, bathroom, five bedrooms, a small back garden and a wooden garage. To the rear of the property was a service road that led from Grafton Road. It served a small factory called The Art Marble Works. Grafton Road itself had about six shops past the service road, but the one I remember most keenly was Edward's, our paper shop. Now, of course, it has all been replaced by the multi-storey car park.

'In 1938, when we moved, I was nine years old. It was in New Malden that I was to find my first true friend. He was fourteen-year-old George Norris. He used to pull a large baker's barrow and he asked me one day if I'd like a cake. I think he thought I was a little thin and needed feeding up! I teamed up with George and two other boys: Leslie Wilson and Rex Norton. We were all great friends. I suppose we were a bit of a gang. We dared each other to do things as young boys do. One of our dares was to walk the full length of the back wall of the Plaza Cinema. The wall was about twenty-five feet high and eighteen inches wide. I don't remember worrying about falling off, and I'm glad to say we never did. The Plaza had been gutted by fire years before. When we had a little money we'd go to a sweet shop called Cicely's and buy a penny's worth of whatever we fancied, then climb the dome tower on top of the Plaza and watch the shoppers as they passed below. Cicely's was opposite the Plaza and situated next to the old Sainsbury's. Sainsbury's itself isn't there now, it's a video hire shop. During the war, in 1942, a bomb landed in the middle of the road right outside this sweet shop. Another bomb dropped outside the Railway Inn on the same road. The pub is under the railway, beside the arch. I remember climbing down into the craters afterwards looking for bits of shrapnel.

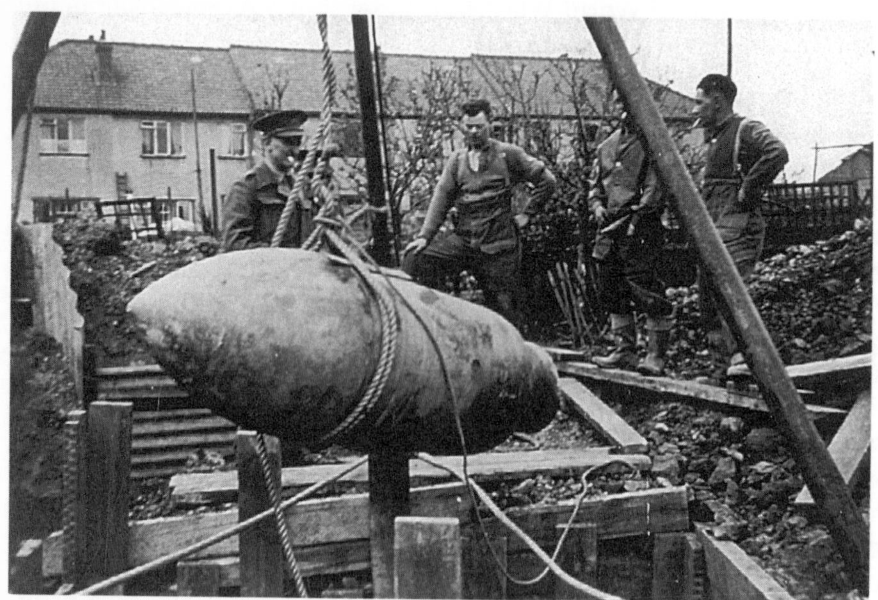

Unexploded German bomb recovered from 9 Woodstock Way, Mitcham, 1940s. *(Paul Wood)*

'My Dad thought it better to move away from the proximity of the station, so we found a house in Cambridge Road. The rent here was also a pound a week. The far end of this road was also bombed. We were lucky and missed the worst, but an incendiary bomb did land on our roof and burn the rafters. Afterwards we had a new slate roof. When the bombs dropped at the far end of Cambridge Road, my friend, Les Wilson, who lived down there, lost his home. Mum let him stay with us for a while.

'My brother, who was five years older than me, started work as a driver for a general store called Denhams in the early 1940s. The store was situated on the corner of Kingston Road. Later, he joined the RAF as a flight mechanic. It was about this time that the gang cycled over to Hampton Court, near Molesey Lock. Nearby was an amusement arcade. The roller shutter had a notice on it that read, "Closed for D of PE". This meant it was closed for the duration of the present emergency (the war). The lock on the shutter was missing so we pushed the shutter up a bit and rolled under. To us, we'd found ourselves a private little Aladdin's Cave. Lots of rifles, no bullets and plenty of other goodies to play with.

'There was a garage on the corner of Cleveland Road and Kingston Road that was called Paddy's Garage. Before that, there were two Victorian semis. The gang used to keep stray cats in there. We made sure that we fed them daily, until they escaped, that is. The other garage nearby was next to the bridge on Kingston Road. It was called The Rose Garage. It was struck by a thunderbolt and was replaced by the Jet petrol station. The Rose Garage was where I used to fill my motorcycle with petrol, using old, wind-up pumps. Dad bought me my first motorcycle in 1944. It cost him £50 and was a 1937 Empire Star, 350cc.

'My schooling had been at Beverley Central School. The headmaster, if I recall correctly, was Mr Heal. When I left to start work, I was taken on at Smith's bookstall on Surbiton Station. Funnily enough, my brother's first job had been at Smith's bookstall in Shoreham Airport. I had to cycle there every day and start work at six in the morning. I did most of the general work, helping the manager for 13/6d per week. In 1943, I was allowed to mark up the papers. If the paper boys didn't turn up to do their rounds, I had to go out and deliver in their stead. After three months of this, I changed my job. For two weeks I packed and weighed tea and sugar in The International Stores in Malden High Street, opposite the Abbey National bank. Then I changed job again. For several months, I worked at the Luco Art Metal Company on the bypass near Shannon Corner, next door to the What0 cafe. This is now a flyover area with a Tesco's supermarket. The What0 was a transport cafe. At Luco, I was drilling and filing cones that fit at the bottom of tripod camera lenses. This was my part of the war effort. Not far away was the Odeon cinema, our main source of entertainment. The factories nearby were Shannons' and Reid & Sirgrest. This site is now occupied by MFI and Sainsbury's Homebase.

'After the war had ended, our old house, 3 Malden Road, and all around was knocked down to make way for two new office blocks. During the building of one on our home site, I asked the foreman if I could go up on the outside lift to take some photographs from the top. He gave me permission and even though it was a grey day, in both senses of the word, I managed a few pictures with my old Brownie Box camera.

'I spent ten years in the RAF between 1946 and 56 then had a few other jobs before marrying my wife Jean, a Thames Ditton girl, in 1958. I then worked for BOAC/BA as an aircraft engineer from 1966 to my retirement in 1991. We're now retired and enjoying our lives together.'

9

Epsom and Cheam

Times were very very different sixty or more years ago. These four contrasting accounts are of considerable interest for the varying social conditions encountered in Surrey's earlier years. It was very much a case of "them and us" and the gentry were held in considerable esteem.

Elizabeth Gimlette's parents moved from Bath to Epsom in 1930, when she was just six years old. 'They moved to share a house with one of my father's brothers, who had just become a widower. Number 15 St Martin's Avenue was a very large house. Once, it had been the vicarage for the nearby St Martin's Church. My uncle, who was always impetuous, bought the house without getting a proper building survey carried out, so the family subsequently incurred large bills for the clearance of all the blocked drains! The house stood surrounded by its garden. There was a large lawn that was used for the playing of bowls, several fruit trees at one end, a rockery, flower beds and a small kitchen garden beside the gardener's shed. Next to the shed was a water butt. To one side of the house was a long, narrow driveway, which led to a garage. Inside the garage, a boarded floor had been laid and a turntable set in it. The car, therefore, an Armstrong Siddeley driven by my mother, never had to be reversed up the driveway, it was simply turned around within the garage interior by means of a switch and lever at the side.

The house had a resident cook, two young housemaids and a governess for my sister and myself. A sewing woman came in once a week to do the mending, and a gardener also came in to help my uncle outdoors once a week. We were well looked after! My father worked on his book, *A Dictionary of Malayan Medicine*, and my mother ran the house and household. She made cakes on the cook's afternoons off. During the three years that I lived at St Martin's Avenue, until

1933, there were stables at the end of the road. Because our governess had a "young man" there, the afternoon walks we took with her always began or ended with a visit to the stables. We fed the horses in their stalls with sugar lumps while the governess talked to her young man. Later these same stables became a garage. Alongside there was an alleyway that was a quick cut-through to the church and the town. Opposite number 15, named Hillside by my parents, was Timberhatch, where our friends lived. Their house was relatively new with an open-plan front garden. Having no fencing was quite an innovation in those days and it was predictable, my parents said, that any passing dogs would make use of the soft ground! As one faced this house from the road, the next one along belonged to Mrs Piper, mother of the artist John Piper. She was an elderly, kind lady and we were sometimes taken to have tea with her. The real pleasure of this outing was to play afterwards in her large, rambling garden that held a revolving summerhouse. You simply turned it to face the sun! Timberhatch is still there, but the land between the two houses is now a tennis court and the other strip of garden has been sold and built upon.

Another outing was to the Epsom market, held on Saturday mornings. The stalls were all set around the base of the clock tower. This still continues today. We mainly went there to buy fruit and vegetables, and I always remember my uncle bidding lustily for bunches of bananas! Another treat was to be taken to have tea at Riddington's Tea Shop in the High Street, with its bow windows, leaded glass panes and curved, cushioned window seats. Riddington's was called Barnard's Shop when my father was at school at Epsom College on the Downs in 1880. Riddington's closed, about ten years ago, I think.

My sister and I went to a small private school in a cul-de-sac known as The Pavement. This school was run by two unmarried ladies. Miss Rhoda and Miss Babs Hamilton-Pott. During the summer term, we had a sports day that was held in the garden at the back – a grand occasion! On Friday evenings, every week without fail, my uncle and parents went to the Epsom Cinema to see the current film being shown. Some were better than others I gathered, but it didn't matter what was on. This was their one night out. It was in 1934 that my parents moved to Cheam, when my uncle announced his intention to marry. Our newly built house was 50 York Road, and this is still there today. My sister and I went to a private school called Evensfield, exactly opposite the Sutton High School. Unfortunately, Evensfield has now closed down. During 1935/6, Sutton and Cheam became a borough. There was great excitement, with many mementoes sold in all the shops. I recall that at that time a crested teaspoon appeared in our home. My sister and I had now progressed to riding push bikes and we often went to the chalk hills at Banstead. We cycled through Belmont village, crossed over the Brighton road and then turned right through the bus park and alongside the railway line till we reached the switchback slopes of chalk, which are still pushing up here in the Downs. They are in two groups. A small bridge crosses the railway to more humpbacked hills that lie along the other side. These hills and dips were a great cycling experience!

It was around this time that green roofing tiles appeared on the roofs of new houses. The general opinion was that these tiles were strange and inappropriate. In 1936, when I was twelve years old, my mother had to sell the house in York Road as my father had died quite suddenly, only two months after we'd taken possession. Thereafter, I sadly no longer lived in Surrey.'

'I remember Derby Day when I look back to my childhood. It was always considered a great event and gave you the chance to dress up if you had money. Unfortunately, my family was quite poor and we never had any money, let alone money to spare for going to the races! So, as a child, I'd remove my shoes to run amongst the other kids as they shouted at the posh people travelling in their carriages to the Epsom Downs. If we were lucky and the travellers felt pity for us, they'd throw out their small change and we'd fight over it in the middle of the road. It was fun, but dangerous. I cut my elbow badly one year when I was knocked down. I needed stitches, but my mother wouldn't take me to hospital. But how I loved to see the ladies all dressed up in their finery and feathery hats. They'd carry dainty umbrellas with frills or wave little decorated fans. The gentlemen were neatly groomed, dressed in dark suits with top hats and carried canes. How I wished to be rich!'

Margaret Storey came to live in Cheam in 1930. 'My family lived in Cecil Road and was in earshot of the Southern Railway and also the roaring moan of traffic that was the Kingston bypass, now the A217. I remember that behind our house was a large field in which sheep and cows were allowed to graze. It joined the base of our garden, then rose in a slope up to the bypass. On the opposite side of that busy road was Cheam School and its surrounding playing fields, edged with rows of swaying elms that were homes to noisy, nesting rooks and crows. I remember that they were active birds. Forever busy, forever circling, calling out. At the bottom of our garden, where it joined the field, we had a stout pole that was the wireless aerial pole. Most of the houses along our road had these, with thin cables stretching the length of the garden up to the eaves of the house. Whenever we wanted to go shopping we'd go to Malgrave Road or into Cheam Village. I enjoyed the grocers' shops, with their glass-topped biscuit tins and sacks of coffee and maize on the floor. Also, there would be bundles of kindling that smelt wonderfully of pine. Sometimes, the grocer would give children broken biscuits. Loose biscuits were available back then. Then there was the dairy shop, that smelt very strongly of milk but with a sour undertone.

Aeroplanes were quite rare. We used to look up to the sky and point, shouting, "It's a monoplane! They're more rare than biplanes!" Mother used to take me to Croydon for a "half-crown flip". The earth would slowly spin and tilt beneath. It was wonderful, amazing and hardly believable. Cheam Station had been intended as a junction, with more platforms, which is why it is unnaturally wide. It cost a penny a mile to travel in the thirties and Sutton was just a mile away. From the "Up" platform, one early morning during the war, just before daybreak, I watched the transit of Venus behind the moon.

'Cheam Village had many more shops and we all went there the most often. In the High Street, a cobbler sat cross-legged in the window of his shop, and it was there that we took our shoes for repair. Sometimes the cobbler would chat, but sometimes he could be most curt and not answer anyone's questions. But I liked to watch him work, it seemed an easy skill. There was a cinema in the station road that was a huge, concrete building. Many of the shops and businesses have not changed. Clubs and the local Sunday School performed their plays in the Town Hall. I was in one once, playing a small doll in a production called *The Smallest Doll*. I never understood the play at all, but I enjoyed watching my friends perform when they were in productions. Whilst my family lived in Cheam, we witnessed the lovely surrounding fields changing into housing estates. There was a big house opposite Cheam School that fell into decay and was pulled down so they could build a block of flats. A road made a loop through the field at the bottom of our garden, so instead of elms, sheep and cows, we had noise and the staring back walls of semi-detached houses.

'My godmother lived in Epsom. To visit her, I would walk through Nonsuch Park. This absolutely amazes me now. It seems like such a long way! Autumn was the most interesting season because we girls would collect the conkers and use them to make furniture in our dolls' houses. We'd stick pins in them to make legs, and another four to make the chair's back, which we would then interweave with wool. Naturally though, many of the girls and boys used to use them for fighting. Nonsuch Park then was usually pronounced "None-Such", after Henry VIII's famous palace there. This was probably in a state of decay when Charles II gave it to one of his mistresses, for she sold it for scrap. It seems a shame that we were deprived of a palace.

'My cousin lived in Onslow Village, just outside Guildford, below the Hog's Back. It was quite different with its chalky upland, for a start. It also seemed a very open place. Sound carried further and more sharply, they had beech hedges and not privet. Behind their house, a field rose so steeply to the Hog's Back that my aunt and uncle believed it could never be built upon. They were right for a long time. It's unfortunate that London swallowed up Wimbledon, where I now live, otherwise I'd still be living in Surrey.'

"Frank" relived his childhood for me, but preferred to remain anonymous. 'My cousin, Percy, and I went to school at the same time. It was 1905, and we were both five years old and lived in the same street. My mother was his father's sister. Percy and I were close, which is surprising considering you couldn't find two children more different from each other. Each year you'd move up a class, and each class had an upper and lower division. I was always in the lower division, but that in itself was not surprising since I was hardly ever there. Percy was an excellent scholar and enjoyed schooling and sports. I couldn't take the discipline. It was very strict at Malden. I spent my days when I should have been at school wandering down by the Thames, playing in fields, or, if I got hungry, dodging any policemen so that I could get to the sweet shop and pinch a sweet from one of the open jars.

'My father worked hard and was very Victorian in nature. He thought nothing of giving me the cane or slipper. He worked for the brewery and often came home with a bottle of something. My mother was a housewife and very proud of our home. If she wasn't polishing some obscure piece of furniture, she was darning a sock or baking a loaf of bread. Unfortunately, when I think of those times and try to remember them, all I remember of my mother is seeing her straining over the old mangle in the kitchen, wringing out clothes. In our house we had a music room, a room I was not allowed to go into except on special occasions such as birthdays or Christmas. There was a small piano in there that my mother used to play and sometimes she'd sing. Father would sit next to her smoking his pipe. I think I was about ten when my father lost his job and we became very poor. Percy's family used to help us out as much as they could but they had their own family to feed. Father was too proud to ask for charity or help, so I often went out last thing at night to steal a chicken or some eggs from a local house that kept them in their back garden. I never felt guilty for stealing. They had a big house and seemed well off and that food was for our survival. Anyway, mother dug out a small kitchen garden in the back and began to grow her own vegetables – potatoes, carrots, that sort of thing. Sometimes mother and I used to go to Kingston market to buy cheap food, usually late in the day, but if I was quick and daring enough I could usually snatch an item or two off a stall and put it in my pocket. I became quite an adept little thief.

'Tram lines were laid down in our road and it soon became obvious that we couldn't stay living where we were. We had to move. Cheam was our destination. We got ourselves a tiny flat above a butcher's shop. We shared with another family. We had the middle floor; the Walkers had the top floor. We shared the kitchen and the bathroom. I had to buck my ideas up and behave. There were too many watchful eyes about. Father got himself a milk round and finally we had a solid income coming in. Mother took us back to Kingston on the tram one year to buy me some shoes for the forthcoming winter. I think this was 1912, or thereabouts. The shop was Aylott's. I don't know why I remember that name, but I do. Father nailed the Blakeys on to the bottom one evening, and I remember tap dancing in the kitchen on the linoleum floor.

'Our family was churchgoing and I had to go to Sunday school morning and afternoon, then in the evening we would all go to evensong. Even listening to the preacher I never felt guilty for stealing when I did. I believe I did it to help my family survive through difficult times. During Harvest Festival, my mother would make loaves of bread and take along flowers to the church. As my school years came to an end, many of the local horses and wagons had disappeared and been replaced by motor cars or trams. The fields were going rapidly as new houses began to be built. I left school with an appalling education.

'It wasn't until many years later that I felt guilty about wasting my life as a child. During the Second World War, I learned that Percy had been killed. He'd been shot. He'd been such a good kid, educated, polite, keen to learn, whilst I'd done as little as possible and was ambling my way through life. Percy's death turned my life around. I became a fireman and worked solidly for thirty-five years. I had to retire due to ill health and took up a librarian's job. I spent many of my home hours educating myself. I may have started life a rascal, but for Percy, I'll end it well.'

10

Mitcham Memories

Mitcham is another traditional Surrey town, famous for its lavender and once an idyllic rural retreat. Here we have accounts from two Mitcham ladies, one the daughter of a local family, the other originally from London.

Mrs Ellen Hall was born in Mitcham. Along with her parents, Ellen lived in a tiny flat with one brother and four other sisters.

'It was rather cramped and with no private amenities. We shared with our neighbours. It was quite a relief to start school and have a bit of space. I went to Gorange Park School. It was a co-ed. I learnt the three Rs there and was forced to do PE. I didn't like sport. I left Gorange when I was fourteen and went on to higher education at a school on the Links Road. I learnt book-keeping, shorthand and typing there – lots of secretarial duties. I also took a keen interest in first aid and was a volunteer with the St John's Ambulance network. I finally got a job in accounts at the Ronson Lighters company on the Strand. Eventually, though, another Ronson office opened in Leatherhead and I transferred there. It was closer for me and quicker. I'd learnt to drive by then, and when I bought my first car it was a Morris Eight. While I worked, I was also helping out at my parents' newsagents on York Road in Wandsworth. I always kept busy and prided myself on being able to do so. Then in 1937 I got married at St Faith's. My husband worked as a master builder. Life was going well until the war began.

'I started working more and more at my parents' shop, and doing less travelling to Leatherhead. The petrol was rationed and very expensive. Taxi drivers had limit curfews, so they were of no use to me. My St John's Ambulance training came in very handy when the bombs began dropping. First, the Germans had what we called flying bombs. You'd be walking down the street and you would hear the planes coming and run for cover. I remember once, I was wearing my tin helmet when a bomb was dropped. I hid in a ditch behind a wall of sandbags and cried as all this shrapnel and bits of wood rained down upon my head. It was terrifying. We didn't think it could get much worse, but it did. The Germans had doodlebugs. Horrific things that you could hear coming, but which then went silent. Frequently I got down on my knees and prayed that it would drop anywhere else but on me. I was very lucky. I trained as an Air Raid Warden and frequently found myself patching up people with shrapnel injuries. I also did a fire watch. You took turns in two-hour stints, carrying pails of water, your helmet and a first-aid kit. It was very tiring as I worked feverishly away on the stirrup pumps, pumping the water through.

SC/V/2

BOARD OF TRADE

SUPPLEMENTARY CLOTHING BOOK.

This book must not be used until the holder's name, full postal address and National Registration Number have been written below.

Holder's Name WALTER RONALD COX
(in BLOCK letters)
Address 134 WORPLESDON ROAD
(in BLOCK letters)
STOUGHTON. GUILDFORD

NATIONAL REGISTRATION No.
D.M.O. / 4177064 /

KEEP THIS BOOK SAFE. If it is lost, it will not be possible to replace it.

See Instructions overleaf.

Page 1

NH 2394068 NH 2394068

Motor Fuel Ration Book

MOTOR CAR
1501 – 2200 C.C.
14 – 19 H.P.

Registered No. of Vehicle
Registered No. of Vehicle
Date and Office of Issue
Date and Office of Issue

This book is the property of Her Majesty's Government

Instructions to Issuing Clerks
See that the issue of this Ration Book is Recorded on the applicant's registration book.

This portion, after completion, to be detached and forwarded to the Regional Petroleum Officer with Form P 2218

The coupons in this book authorise the furnishing and acquisition of the number of units of motor fuel specified on the coupons.

Ration books

'Everybody was so happy when the war ended. We held a street party. All the neighbours were invited and we all used our rations to put together a tremendous feast for everyone. It was amazing where all the food came from. We all looked out for one another. Helped wherever and however we could. I remember the first Christmas after the war, the milkman mentioned that he'd not seen his children for three months as they were living up in Scotland with his wife's relatives. I volunteered to do his round for him so he could catch the train up north. Anyone would do things like that. I got up at three and did the round in the freezing weather, but I was happy to do it.' Our interview was suspended at this point to allow Mrs Hall to take a telephone call from her daughter in faraway Canada. When we resumed, Ellen was quite emotional about the old times with her husband, who has since passed away.

'For a treat, my husband and I bought a motorbike and we used to go touring down in Devon and Cornwall. We never had a sidecar, we thought them extremely out of touch! So I always used to ride pillion. We never went very fast. There was no danger. It was great fun. If we wanted to celebrate an occasion, we never went out. After the war, it was enough just to be able to stay at home, put on the wireless, cook a nice meal and relax with some dancing in the living room lamplight afterwards. Soon enough, though, I became quite busy with my two daughters. I still helped out at the shop and manned the St John's tent at any of the local fairs, but my time was mostly taken up with my husband and children. The family was so important to people then. Family used to be everything. Keeping the family unit together was crucial.'

I asked Ellen about healthcare for her large family. 'Well, I can laugh about it now, but we used to do it all wrong back then. Our family never, ever, called the doctor. It wasn't worth it. We were a large family that needed feeding and it didn't do to have to give away a ration of our food to pay for medical care. If we had colds or the flu, you soldiered on. You took the weird home remedies that mother gave out and carried on working. I don't know what she made them with, I never dared ask, but it tasted horrible. I recall once my sister had a bad stomach ache. As usual, we didn't call out a doctor. She still did her chores. But it got worse, she was in a lot of pain. In the end, Mum relented and out came the doctor. Turned out she had appendicitis.'

These memories are so very important to a woman such as Ellen Hall. She is now blind and spends her life in a nursing home. 'At least I'm not blind to my memories,' she said.

Joyce Arnold, a lady who herself is a keen historian, was kind enough to share with me some of her own memories. 'The first thing I recall about Surrey is the day my family moved from London and into Mitcham. It was 1924, I think, and Mitcham was definitely a place in the countryside. At least, it was then. My father was out in the removal van and I remember walking with my mother, who at that time was pushing my younger brother in his pram. We walked through a new housing estate and the road we were on was made of railway sleepers, but beneath, oozing black mud seeped through. There were many new roads being built just then, but there was no local school anywhere in the vicinity. Fortunately, two enterprising ladies started a private school in their three-bedroomed house. When I was old enough, I went there. The downstairs front room and the three bedrooms were used as classrooms, but the back room, with its French windows, was used for dancing, singing and morning assembly. Our cloakroom was the kitchenette and, of course, the garden was used as our playground. Before the new council school was built, about forty boys and girls had their education there.

'It was 1932 when I enrolled at Mitcham County School for Girls. It was a fair distance and I had to walk across Mitcham Common every day. There were no buses and my parents did not have a car. I enjoyed the walks and I loved reciting homework to the others as we went along! A multitude of brightly-coloured gorse bushes adorned the common, and with the larks soaring above our heads, singing at the summer, it was a wonderful time. There were the other times, though, when I had to walk through snow blizzards and tentatively step through the fog, not forgetting the many thunderstorms, which always began just as it was home time. On the common was a place called Seven Islands Pond, a constant and favourite source of my interest. When it was frozen over, we could skate upon its glassy surface, and in spring take home jars of frogspawn to analyse.

'During this time Mitcham became a borough, and it was a grand occasion to be on the Fair Green with all the other school children when Mr Mizen, a nurseryman, was made the town's first mayor. Each child was given a lavender-coloured pottery mug emblazoned with the new coat of arms. The Fair Green was a very much used place for social occasions. I remember going there in August and watching the grandfather of one of my cousins play cricket for the county.

'Eventually, I moved away from Mitcham and for the next ten years or so, including the war years, I lived in other places. Then, in 1945, I returned as a newly married lady and lived in Lower Kingswood. It was a pleasant village at the top of Reigate Hill. I had all the shops my husband and I required and there was an abundance of village activities. I enjoyed the Surrey countryside greatly. Involving myself in the village life, I made many new friends and brought up three sons.'

A Mitcham-bound London Transport bus, No 44, in the Balham underground station. Many died from drowning whilst sheltering in the Tube station as water poured in from a broken water main. *(Paul Wood)*

11

The Glorious Twelfth

Many associate "The Glorious Twefth" with the start of the grouse-shooting season but in Meacham it has always been an equally important date – marking the opening of Mitcham Fair.

The following account was kindly sent to me by Mr John Elwin. It details his early childhood and a great fascination of his life, the Mitcham Fair.

'I was born in Mitcham in 1923 at Gorringe Park and lived in a house just off the main London Road, not far from the Tooting border. As a young boy I would watch the changeover point in Tooting, where the trams would switch from the electrical underground pickup to the overhead wires, enabling them to continue their journey through Mitcham. There was a man that was employed full-time to do this procedure. Tooting was quite a built-up area with many houses and shops – it was part of the London area – but Mitcham was different. Soon after crossing the boundary towards Mitcham, there was a lot of open space. On the left was Figges Marsh, unfenced and open to the public for recreation purposes. On the right was a burial ground, and further up from that was another recreation ground. On it were a chalet and a bandstand. On summer evenings concert parties were held. I recall that the Mitcham Gas Works Band would play there.

'The roads in those days were all gas-lit, as was the house in which I lived. Looking back now, I realise times were hard for many people living here. Despite all this, I had a happy childhood. Kids made their own amusement. I remember we couldn't afford a wireless, so we made do with an old wind-up gramophone. We had no cinemas in Mitcham, we had to go into Tooting, where there were several.

'I started school in 1928, at Gorringe Park Central School in Sandy Lane, about half a mile away from my house. To get there, I would walk along the stream in Figges Marsh. This stream has since been piped underground. To the left of this stream was a large piece of land owned by the Searle family, who were travelling showmen. It was here that they lived in caravans and kept all their fairground equipment. They had been there many years, and every year they would set up a small holiday fair for Easter, Whitsuntide and August Bank Holiday. Their old, steam-driven switchbacks (roundabouts with two hills and a rail track), fair organs, rides and steam traction engines had a fascination for me.

'The school in Sandy Lane was in three sections, infants', juniors' mixed and the boys' school, all with separate playgrounds. I dreaded starting school, but it was better than I thought it would be at first. The headmistress was a Miss Marlow, a very kind lady. I think that all the teachers in the infants' school were ladies. In particular, I also seem to remember a Miss Jarvis. Sometimes we would assemble in the main hall where there was a piano. From there we would file off to our classrooms to the march tune of *Men of Harlech*. Next came the mixed juniors' where the headmaster was a Mr Crawley. The other teachers' names were Mr Baker and Mrs De-Voil. Punishment for wrongdoing was not uncommon. We were given the cane for serious offences, but usually we were rapped on the wrist or punched in the shoulder. Discipline was strict. If you were absent, the school board man was at your house that very day to find out why! Milk was supplied for the pupils to drink at school in the mornings. Dinners were provided for the teachers but not for the pupils. We all went home for ours.

'At the age of eleven, girls left Gorringe Park for the Links Road School. In 1934, we moved to another part of Mitcham known as Lonesome. The place got its name because it was a remote part of East Mitcham, and was mainly fields owned by the Mizen family, the local market garden growers. Pain's Firework Factory was also located here. I was still attending Gorringe Park and was now in the boys' school. The headmaster was a Mr Plowright. The other teachers were Mr Jenkins, who taught sport; Mr Toller, who taught music; Mr Blackburn, who taught science; Mr Carter, who taught woodwork; and Mr Swift, Mr Peek, Mr Bailey, Mr Cox and Mr De-Voil. There was no official uniform. Most boys wore a striped belt in school colours, with an "S" fastening hook, school cap and blazer. In 1934, we were all given a presentation lavender china beaker decorated with a coat of arms. The colour represented the lavender grown here in the old days. This was because Mitcham Urban District was to become the Borough of Mitcham. All of the teachers from all of the Mitcham schools escorted their pupils to the cricket green, opposite the vestry hall, to hear the Proclamation of Charter Day. Seated on the cricket green, we heard all the various speeches. The new mayor was a Mr Chart, an old Mitcham man, well into his eighties. In an amusing part of his speech about Mitcham he said, "It ain't all lavender", referring to the slums.

'Indeed, Mitcham was an area of contrasts. With a large common and golf course, some parts were quite countrified. The cricket green has a history that goes back over three hundred years! There are built-up areas with factories, and an old gas works and paint works. We had a large gypsy population then, as they were attracted here by the annual fair in the old days. They also got work in the lavender fields. Many travelling showmen bought up the workyards for their winter quarters and depots.

The Proclamation of Charter Day was fine and sunny with crowds of people watching the long procession of floats moving slowly through the town centre to the cricket green. One of the local showmen, Harry Gray, had a fair in his yard near the town centre. In the evening, there was a large fireworks display given by Pain's Fireworks.

'In July 1937, I reached the age of fourteen, time to leave school and start employment. A prospect I did not look forward to.'

I have been helped in piecing together the next parts of John's recollections by Mr David Cooper of Sussex.

'The last time the Mitcham fair was held on the old fair green was 1923, the year of my birth. Nearly everyone in Mitcham attended the fair, as did a great many people from the London area. The first sign of the fair coming to Mitcham was soon after the bank holiday, then the first Monday in August. The showmen's road trains would be moving in from sites such as Hampstead Heath. Usually, we kids would we playing cricket on Figges Marsh as this was the school holidays. The steam traction engines could be heard, pulling three or four wagons each, blowing their shrill steam whistles. The cricket game would be abandoned, and excitedly we'd all run over to see which rides would be at the fair. Many would be Harry Gray's loads moving to his local yard to await the pull on. (Moving on to the site.) The others would pull into Searle's by the side of the marsh.

'In those days, an old custom at fair time was an excuse for kids to get money to spend at the fair. It was called Spare A Penny For The Grotto. All over Mitcham, grottoes would be built on pavements, with oyster shells and broken pottery used to make caves. A piece of mirrored glass would be laid down to simulate a lake, and would be decorated with flowers pinched from a local garden. We would then wait for passers-by and demand a spare penny for the grotto. While all this grotto building was going on, the council workers would be preparing the fair site on the Three Kings Piece.

'The grass on the site was seldom cut and would be thickly mixed with clovers. By early August the ground would be swarming with grasshoppers. This was the time to watch the marking out, where the grounds would be marked out with chalk to indicate different sites for the various rides that were coming. Each pitch was staked and numbered, and in total there were usually about four hundred and fifty sites. It was quite a task to set out. By 9 August the work would be completed. The showmen were allowed two days to build up their rides or stalls, and on 10 August we would get up early in the morning to walk from Gorringe Park along the London Road towards the fair green. Many of the traction engines still moving towards the site stopped at the Three Kings Pond to take on water. The seventeen-acre site became a hive of activity. On the railway side of the ground, the big machines were sited and took up about half of the site.

'O'Brien's switchback got an early start. The eight dragon cars were hoisted up on to the hill tracks and coupled up. Other machines being built up were the Wilson's Rodeo switchback, Gray's steam yachts, Bird's yachts, the gallopers (horse carousel) of George Irvin, together with Pettigrove's gallopers, O'Brien's gallopers, Fred Gray's gallopers and Harry Gray's gallopers; there were two cakewalks, many dodgem tracks, lightening swirls, Noah's arks, a waltzer, helter-skelter, ghost-trains and chairoplanes. In the late thirties new machines appeared such as Proctor's airways, autodromes and the Monte Carlo speedways. Harry Gray had his Coronation Ben Hur at the fair in 1937, an impressive machine built by Lakins. By the morning of 11 August, the fair was nearing completion.

'The shows were placed alongside the beehive bridge. There was The Great Show by Tom Norman, two boxing booths and the Wild West show of Wally Shufflebottom, known as Wally Texan by many. Captain Purchese had his Wild Lion show and Mr Barry had his Wall of Death show where he and a real live lion would ride the wall. There was a Globe of Death, a small circus, a flea circus, freak shows and many striptease shows.

'Then, scattered intermittently, were the coconut shies, round stalls, juvenile roundabouts and swing boats. The empty wagons would be pushed out of the way, and sometimes we kids were asked to help. This we'd do willingly, in the hope of a free ride as payment. When the fair was all built up, the final job was to lay all of the cables underground and to fit large, white bulbs on the big machines. The musical organs would be tuned. I remember, in particular, a strong man who gave exhibitions before the fair opened by bending metal bars and passing round a hat to his audience. The showmen would relax in the nearby pubs the day before the big opening. They would hope for three days of fine weather. But they were lucky to get them. We had many wet Mitcham fairs!

'On the Glorious Twelfth, the Mitcham Fair would open to the public. The showmen worked continuously, polishing brass and accepting deliveries of coal and water. The show landladies were busy making the famous Mitcham Fair rock, attracting onlookers as the rock was slung over a hook and stretched. This was repeated many times until the texture was right. Then it would be cut into strips and sold to the onlookers for a penny a time whilst it was still warm. The toffee apples were made there, too, and I remember the distinctive smell and taste of burnt toffee.

'Shortly before twelve noon, a large group of council officials would turn up and mount the stage with prominent showmen. Tom Norman would be in dress suit and bow tie at the microphone. As the awnings were being taken down from the gallopers, the organ engines would turn the wheels at the back by belts and the showmen would wait for the sign to insert the cardboard music books into the keyframes. Newsreel cameramen would shoot the scenes in front of the show, and journalists would take notes for their respective stories.

The speeches would be made and the mayor would be introduced. Then Tom Norman would raise three cheers from the crowd for the mayor, and the golden key would be held aloft as two silver bells would ring. This was the showmen's signal. All the music started up at once, steam whistles would blow and the noise would be terrific. The fair was now open!

'The official party would make their way to O'Brien's Golden Dragons, which would be bedecked with hanging baskets of flowers. The mayor, with the golden key and the officials, would board the switchback for a thrilling ride, then the children were finally allowed on for free. Paper streamers and confetti were thrown over the cars by the showmen, then the organ would strike up and music blared out. It was all a wonderful cacophony of sight and sound. After the first ride, a charge of four pence was to be made per ride. The Golden Dragon machine was magnificent with its marble pillars, a large musical organ and a waterfall at the back. The dragon cars had five benches, each covered in red velvet. The cars had dragon heads with a tongue in the mouth. As the ride moved, the tongue would sway back and forth.

'Buses and trams were extra full during fair time. They came from Tooting and London, the people in Mitcham would walk. Most people entered the fair at the Pond Entrance. The coconut shies would do good business. If you didn't want a coconut you could ask for a different prize instead. To get to the big rides you always had to pass through the smaller stalls such as the hooplas, skittles, spinners, darts and wheel 'em ins. At this stall, your penny had to land on a numbered square. There were also one-armed bandits and a game where you could throw your penny on a prize. I managed this one year and won a George V box of chocolates. Imagine my surprise upon returning home to find the box filled with mildew-covered chocolates. I wondered at the time how may fairs that box had seen. Still, I saw the funny side.

'Most of my money was spent on my favourite rides, the switchbacks. The gallopers were second favourite. I was only allowed six shillings to spend during the whole three days of the fair, so I could never sample everything that took my fancy. I once went on the Joy Wheel. This was a wooden disc, highly polished, on which the riders sat. As the disc picked up speed, you'd get thrown off. The showmen called this a “Oncer”. Probably because few people ever rode this a second time. In 1933, the first waltzer came to the show, owned by Thurstons. After that, many more modern machines came to the show.

‘The best time to visit the fair was in the evening. People would descend from all around as this was the biggest fair in the south of England. The fair green would be alive with people arriving and departing. You had quite a job sometimes just to get from one ride to another. Each show had a loud tannoy system, showmen beating drums or symbols in time with the organ music. There was the sound of the guns from the rifle ranges, and bells on the strikers added to the wail of sound. A lot of the coconut stalls had naphtha flares and flying flags. The light from the fair was brilliant, with steam and smoke rising into the night sky. This smoky light could be seen for many miles around, and I’m sure the noise could be heard too. After three glorious days the fair would be over. The showmen would move on, leaving the Three Kings Piece littered with rubbish and many wonderful memories of another magnificent fair.’

12

A Surrey Postman

We often take the postman for granted. In all weathers, the post arrives on the doormat, but how often do we think about the stories that our postman can tell? Everybody has a story to tell, as this chapter reveals.

Paul Wood informed me of his family's connection with the Post Office – over two hundred years of service! 'My father, Reginald Frank Carrington Wood, was known as "Chippie" to those he worked with, and as "Jack" to my mother. He was born on 22 April 1896 in Fairview Road, Norbury. During his childhood days he witnessed the introduction of electricity to the Croydon Corporation Trams. These trams terminated at Norbury, on the south side of the railway bridge in London Road. The L.C.C. Trams took over on the north side, where there was an underground pickup. A police station stands there today. One of the schools he was educated at was Stamford Road Boys' School, Norbury. He left school in 1910 and commenced work as a telegram boy messenger and odd-job lad for Smallhakes, the bakers at 1022 London Road, Thornton Heath, opposite the then beautiful Thornton Heath Pond. Telegrams for that area would be phoned through from the Croydon GPO Telegraph Office, written out on an official form, enveloped and then delivered by dad. Later, the messenger boys were taken on by the GPO, and given uniforms from the head offices.

'My father was posted to the Head Post Office in High Street, Croydon. The messengers' entrance and exit was on Middle Street, between Crown Hill and Surrey Street. Telegrams were delivered on foot or by bicycle in a large area that stretched from Norbury in the north, Purley to the south, Norwood to the east and Beddington to the west. The working day of a boy messenger before the First World War was extremely long, with a military-type discipline. The day would start with an inspection of cleanliness. His uniform, boots and leather belt had to be highly "bulled". Brass buttons, cap and collar badges, and his belt buckle had to sparkle. The uniform had to be clean and correctly pressed, the push-bike had to be roadworthy and spotless. No rust or paint chips were allowed. If anything was found to be not up to standard, the inspecting officer would send the boy home and lose him a day's pay. This also happened if you didn't make it to the parade ground on time.

Reginald Frank Carrington Wood – Postman Croydon 59, outside Melfort Road Sorting Office, 1920s. *(Paul Wood)*

'After inspection, a rifle drill lasting thirty minutes would follow. There was a miniature shooting range beneath the sorting office! What shooting a rifle had to do with delivering telegrams I'll never know! This was 1912 and it was later, in 1916, that dad volunteered

Able Seaman Jack Wood *(Paul Wood)*

for the Royal Navy. He became a Chatham Rating and served on the cruiser *HMS Swiftsure* and HMTBDs (His Majesty's Torpedo Boat Destroyers). At that period in time, one couldn't become a postman at the office at which you had recently served, so he was posted to Ashtead. The distance involved between Norbury and Ashtead was great. Dad had early rises and late deliveries so he spent most of the week in digs in Ashtead, and only came home to Norbury on Sundays. Dad's deliveries usually started at seven in the morning and didn't finish until nine at night!

'He soon returned to Croydon and became Croydon Postman Number 59. He served at all the local sorting offices but preferred to be at Thornton Heath. This building wasn't demolished until late 1996. My father had a charmed life, which was strange considering most of the things he got up to. For instance, he had a telegram to deliver very late at night and quite a distance from the office. A passing lorry with a trailing rope was too good an opportunity to pass up. He was flying along behind the lorry, holding the rope as it travelled at its maximum speed of 20mph. The rope entangled itself in the wheels of dad's bike. He was thrown off and lay directly in the path of an oncoming tram. The clever driver quickly dropped his "cowcatcher" grid and scooped him up. My father proudly carried the scars all his life. Leisure hours were spent riding with a club that met at The Plough on Clapham Common. Saturday afternoons were spent as a spectator at the newly-built Herne Hill Cycle Track.

'In 1926, he and two other postmen were recruited at Croydon to become the first three postmen drivers. He was told to report to the Trojan Commercial Vehicle Factory in Richmond Road, Kingston Upon Thames. This later became part of the Hawker Aircraft factory. Trojan cars had until that time been manufactured in Vicarage Road, Croydon. Dad had had no previous driving experience, so was taken around the streets of Kingston for half an hour by a factory foreman from Trojan's. This started his first day in over thirty years of driving a postal van, including six years driving in wartime blackouts and pea-soup smogs. I recall one accident dad was involved in. It upset him greatly. It was the late 1940s and he was driving a Y-Type Morris 10 mail van. He'd stopped to allow passengers to board a tram, but a young Croydon High School girl on her bicycle didn't stop and she hit the back of the van. This was at Thornton Heath Pond. Her face smashed through the rear door window and into the protective wire screens mounted behind the glass for security purposes. Another time, he was stopped for speeding whilst on the London Road, doing 33mph in a 30mph limit. Attending court, dad was fined a few shillings and had his licence endorsed. A lorry driver who was also attending court referred to the state of the arresting policeman's parents' marriage, and was fined several pounds! The speeding offence cost my father his driving allowance pay.

Postman Driver 'Chippie' Wood, Thornton Heath 1925. Trojan 70cc Mail Van
(Paul Wood)

'In the mid-thirties, the Trojan vehicle was exchanged for a Morris Minor side-valve mail van that was to last my dad until after the Second World War. It was his pride and joy! The drivers had to carry out their own repairs and take care of any daily maintenance.

'In 1936, my elder sister was born. My parents had married in 1932. They were living in a flat in Windsor Road, Thornton Heath. Just months after her birth, in November, my parents noticed a deep red glow in the sky. My dad got on his bike and cycled off to investigate. It apparently was caused by a fire at the Crystal Palace. Many thousands of people from Croydon travelled to view the disaster. Dad was upset. Many animals and birds had perished in the flames, along with his beloved Palace. A place that he and my mum had visited many times.

'As the war clouds darkened over Europe, dad, who was too old for call-up, volunteered for fire-watching service. He was also detailed to do similar duties for the GPO. After 3.30am rises for his daily deliveries and split duties, he never seemed to get home before 11pm. This was no joke for my family. I was born right in the middle of the Battle of Britain. It was September 1940 and we were in a house in Greenwood Road, Mitcham. At the time of my birth, an air raid was raging. A bomb dropped on a house in Beech Grove, just a few roads away. The midwife apparently exclaimed at the explosion, "Was that the baby or the b.. bomb?" Fortunately, Mitcham didn't suffer too badly during the Blitz. It was a different story, however, in the summer of 1944!

'Greenwood Road had street shelters built directly on to the road surface. My grandfather, a foreman in the building trade, warned my parents that they were potential death traps. Without any solid foundations, they would collapse like a pack of cards. We therefore used the shelter built underground at the corner of Greenwood Road and Sheewood Park Road. It later became a cellar to the New Ascension Church. But if time was short, we'd dive under the stairs. Apparently, this was the strongest part of the house.

'On 13 June 1944, south Londoners heard a strange, small motorcycle-type noise in the sky, followed by silence then a direct explosion. The first V1 had arrived. The last would be some nine months later. Between those times, 1500 were to fall on south London and its boroughs: Croydon, Mitcham, Sutton, Carshalton and Beddington. Our newly built, private housing estate on Pollard Hill received eight V1s, doodlebugs and buzzbombs in one square mile. The wailing of the siren and the roar in the sky meant a dive under the stairs. Dad would stand at the front gate with his black, Tommy-style tin hat on. These were issued to postmen during the war. Then suddenly he would be beside us. One time, two buzz bombs came down in our road, some 150 yards away. The houses had gone down, the side of Pollard's Hill Infants' School and the street shelters. Consequently, some of our neighbours, whom we'd been talking to only hours earlier, had been killed outright.

'And it went on. Damage repair people were fed whilst they put new tarpaulin on our roof space. It was soon after, in a single day and the following night, that another three buzz bombs landed within 150 yards. In the morning, we saw that our temporary roof, back and front windows, French doors and ceilings had gone. Yet after replacing our roof cover, it was gone again within the next twelve hours. To me, a little boy, the one casualty in all this horrible war was my teddy bear, made out of an old overcoat. The sirens had wailed and in one mad rush downstairs I forgot my teddy. It broke my heart to find poor Ted had been speared with broken glass, suffering the same fate as my little bed, where I had been sleeping only minutes before. Poor Ted lost a leg and had to have extensive first aid to his stomach. It made me cry and I shouted out, not that the Germans could hear me, "I didn't want my little house broken!"

'I was four years old. The food rationing meant nothing to me; I'd never seen a sweet or fresh fruit. I recall neighbours shouting out that there were bananas in the shops. I would be shoved into a pushchair and raced through the streets to purchase two strange-looking, yellow things. My aunt used to send us food parcels from Singapore! In August 1944, my father decided that it was too dangerous and that my mum, sister and I were to be evacuated to Taunton in Somerset. The reason for this decision was an event which occurred one day as my mother and I were going to visit my grandparents, who lived at the top of Pollard's Hill. Our route was a footpath alongside the golf course, roughly where the modern council estate is today, in line with Recreation Close, and up to the steep slope of Pollard's Hill. We had nearly reached the crest when the sirens went off. We heard the familiar spluttering of a V1 and glanced over our shoulders to see a buzz bomb pass over St Helier Hospital, Carshalton. It appeared to be coming straight towards us! My mother threw me to the ground and lay over me for protection. Seconds later, an enormous bang blasted our ears. The bomb had come down on the Mitcham Common, directly at the end of Manor Road. The crater is still visible today. Near to this spot is Windmill Road, where a few years earlier a whole platoon of Home Guards had been blown to kingdom come by a land mine. They had mistaken the shape for a German paratrooper, and it exploded as they rushed towards it.

'After the end of winter 1944, we returned to Mitcham and I started to go to work with my dad in his postal van. I was known to my work mates as "Splinter". The Post Office was one big family. Everyone knew one another's names. If you met another worker, you always felt a special kind of alliance or brotherhood. I mostly enjoyed delivering at Christmas. There were so many parcels, the Post Office had to hire furniture vans and coaches. The parcels would be sorted on the seats throughout the buses, and my dad was like a team leader for the 4 or 6 foreign students they hired as temporary postmen. Usually, these people were training to be doctors and were after some extra cash. The coach would travel down the centre of the road and the students would rush back and forth, taking parcels from my dad and delivering them to the correct house. Practically every house would always be visited. The more unpleasant deliveries as far as I was concerned were all the dead rabbits and pheasants. These could be sent parcel post with just a label around their necks. I hated delivering their poor limp bodies to folk. Dad enjoyed his work and was certainly an institution on his rounds. He'd do a three-week working rota. One week of walking and two weeks of driving, alternating early and late shifts. He loved it all.

'On his early rounds, my father was very much a magpie. He'd notice items besides people's bins and ask if he could take them at the end of his round. My sister and I never went without a bike. They may not have been new, but they were reliable. Many other objects came the same way. Pets and dogs that had been mistreated would be brought home in his delivery bag, their little heads poking out of the top. In 1955, I left school and became an apprentice mechanic at Broadway Motor Company, opposite the Wimbledon Theatre. They were a Vauxhall Bedford dealership and my pay was 19 shillings weekly. Out of this amount I had to purchase my own tools. It wasn't long before I decided that this life wasn't for me and I soon got another job as a messenger boy at Victoria in London, embarking on the same career as my father many years before.'

13

Cobham and Cranleigh

These three recollections take us back to the 1920s – a time just after the First World War when times were very different from nowadays. Older readers may well recall the places described and may even recall the names and faces of the people featured here.

'I was born 1 April 1927 at The Institute, now known as the Downside Sports and Social Club. When I was two, my parents and I moved to 2, The Island. We stayed here until I was nine, then moved again to 9 Downsview Close, where I lived until my marriage in 1946. Our first home had gas lighting downstairs, and to get to bed, we had to use a candle to guide the way. In the kitchen was a black-leaded range, and there was a small, open fireplace in the front reception room. There

1920s bathtime *(Joyce Gardner)*

was only cold water, so if we wanted to bathe, we'd heat kettles of water and fill up the tin bath, which was placed in front of the fire.

'My school was the Downside Church of England School and I stayed there until I was eleven. I believe this school is now known as St Matthew's. There were no uniforms. I joined the school dancing team and we used to travel to different venues. We wore cerise silk dresses with black patent shoes, and the boys had to wear white shirts, cerise ties, black trousers and shoes. Sir Arthur Glyn was our benefactor.

'One teacher that I remember in particular was Miss Whitcombe. She was very small, grey-haired and taught at the infants' school. She was so very kind, and we all loved her to bits. Then there was Miss Powell, the head of the junior school. In contrast to Miss Whitcombe, Miss Powell was strict and severe, but I managed to get on well with her. When not at school, I would pass my evening hours playing hopscotch or skipping, simple pleasures and certainly not expensive. I enjoyed taking part in my school's sports day activities, which took place annually on the local common. I enjoyed the running mostly.

'At the tender age of fourteen I left school to join the big, wide world, and got a job at a grocer's shop. I stayed until I was nineteen. I had to serve the customers their rations and other goods, counting all the coupons that we had to have to obtain our allowances of certain foods: butter, cheese, bacon, eggs, tea and sugar. I had to weigh out the rations ready for the customers.

'I married my husband before he was called up to do service. He had eighteen months to do in the air force. Locally, we had only one shop, a sub-post office that sold most groceries and vegetables, sweets and cigarettes. The post office was part of a house. It had many owners. I remember Fosters owning it when I was a child, then Dicksons. For the last twenty years or so, Jim and Eileen Robinson were there with their two sons. Then they sold the business and moved to Somerset. We haven't had any shops or a post office in Downside since they left. We have nothing! For shopping, you have to go into Cobham.

'During the war, we had an Anderson shelter in our back garden and would rush into it whenever the sirens were sounded. We'd watch the German bombers fly over on their way to London, and the

V1 and V2 rockets, or doodlebugs as we used to call them, passed over this area en route to London, too. They were such dreadful things, it was terrifying. The engines would shut off and then they would either come straight down or they'd go on a few more miles before landing and exploding. I remember watching a most spectacular sight once, when the planes towing the gliders passed over this area with the parachutists. My uncle was one of them and he never returned. My fondest memory was when the war ended and we had a great party. Everybody went wild with delight and there was plenty of singing and dancing in the streets.'

Dorothy Day wrote to me to tell me about her childhood days. 'I was born on 18 August 1925 at 5 Ditton Hill Road, Long Ditton. At the age of five and six, I attended Ditton Hill Infants' School. The headmistress was a Mrs Davies. Our family then moved to Fleece Road, whereupon my father opened a greengrocery shop. From the ages of six until ten, I attended Galloway House School on Brighton Road in Surbiton. It was owned and run by two spinster sisters called Cissie and Maggie Weir. It was a lovely school and I was certainly very happy there. We'd walk or cycle to class. During break times, I remember that the tuck shop used to sell a glass of milk for sixpence, and a Nestlé bar of chocolate would cost a penny. From the of age of ten to sixteen, I was at Clark's College, Maple Road, Surbiton. When war was declared, the school built a shelter in its basement. We'd have our lessons down there. They made us carry our gas masks constantly.

'My family were listening to Mr Chamberlain on the wireless when he declared that we were at war with Germany. It was a Sunday, 11 November 1939. It was just after his address when the sirens sounded. Luckily, it was a false alarm but the people were very frightened and worried. They all stood around talking outside, and many collected spades and shovels to begin digging an air raid shelter on the island in Fleece Road.

'My dad was appointed ARP Post Warden of our local area. He had to wear a white tin hat whilst the other wardens wore black hats. To start with, they manned the telephone in our home, but later they moved to an empty shop a few doors away where they had an underground post. They had to go there whenever there was a red alert. This underground post was next to the public shelter. They delivered all the flat boxes for the gas masks to our home, so we spent many an hour assembling them and putting string on them as well. The wardens fitted the masks at Long Ditton Parish Hall in Ewell Road. Nightly, the wardens patrolled the streets to make sure everyone was blacked out. I'd go and make tea for them and do jigsaws or play darts. Whenever members of the public had to stay in the shelter overnight, I'd make tea for them, too, and sell buns. It wasn't until much later that many had shelters of their own. I often played a "casualty" for training purposes, being hauled out of the shelter on a stretcher during a practice incident.

'Aged fourteen, I joined the WJAC, Women's Junior Air Corps, as did most girls my age. On leaving Clark's College in September 1941, I commenced work as a shorthand typist at Eagle Components Company. They were based in Portsmouth Road, Long Ditton. They were manufacturers of windows, jettison tanks and other various components for an aircraft firm in Portsmouth called Airspeed. Whenever the sirens sounded, the office staff used to run up Portsmouth Road to an underground shelter. We'd hear the doodlebugs flying over the Thames, and sometimes turning and coming back towards us. Christmas was spent quietly with the loved ones that were still with us, many of our relatives were away at war.

'After the war, my parents sold the shop and we moved to a smallholding in West End Esher. Whilst living here, I met my future husband and we married at Esher Church in 1951, holding the reception at Thames Ditton Parish Hall. Rationing was still in force, and we left for a honeymoon in Jersey complete with our ration books! On our return, we bought a house in Long Ditton and now live in Thames Ditton. I wish the traffic was less so that children could play outside the way we used to – boys skating and girls playing with hoops and whip and top. But we would not want to live anywhere else.'

'My grandfather was a blacksmith. His main trade was shoeing the horses from local farms and repairing farm equipment. Life for him was very hard, and he certainly knew his place whenever he had a visit from a member of the passing gentry. He knew never to meet their eyes and always kept his head bowed. He never said more than "Yes, sir". He felt that he could never say "no" to them. One in particular, whom I'm reluctant to name, would make my grandfather shod his horse and then never pay him! He treated my grandfather with disdain and sneered at him for being a commoner. For his fire, grandfather used a sort of fine, dusty coal mixed with some larger pieces. He'd let my father, as a boy, use the bellows to fan the flames and make the forge unbearably hot. My father took over the business after his father had an accident and lost two fingers, but he'd never let us use the bellows. He thought it was dangerous. Double standards! He allowed us to watch the horses being shod, but after seeing huge nails being driven into the horse's hoof, I never watched again.

'After the First World War, our family moved to Cranleigh. As children we were never allowed to miss Sunday School and we always had to wear our best clothes. I recall once having a hole in my best shoes. Mother got some soot from the chimney and smeared my skin so that it didn't show! Lots of people attended church. It was a duty. Some people looked down on our neighbours who never used to go. The services followed the Common Prayer Book. On Good Friday each year, we'd go into the woods nearby and pick daffodils and other flowers so that they could be used to decorate the church. If the gentry came to the church, their names would be listed on the end of a pew, almost like reserved seats.

'In 1922, we had our first car, an Austin 20 Tourer. It was an open-top and we frequently got wet on our day trips out to Shere, Guildford or Haslemere. My brother and I went to Cranleigh's village school and hated every moment of it. The other boys were bullies and very cruel. I frequently played truant, and got a whipping from my father for doing so. During the war, a doodlebug landed on the school whilst it was empty and completely destroyed it. All the children, in our innocence, believed that it meant no more school, ever. How wrong we were!

'I remember my old house with much affection as most people do, thinking of it now through rose -tinted glasses. Then it was terrible. We had two bedrooms upstairs and two rooms downstairs. There was an open fire in one room, but it was rarely lit and so the house was always freezing, especially in winter. Our bedroom window was broken and we'd patched it up with a piece of cardboard, but still a chill used to infiltrate our little bodies. The house was lit by a single oil lamp that my father used to keep next to his chair so that he could read and smoke his pipe. In the kitchen, my mother always kept a fresh canteen of water for washing or cooking or drinking. There was an old, rusty mangle in the kitchen that she used most Mondays. To iron the clothes, she'd place a plank of wood between the backs of two chairs for balance and then cover it with an old blanket. The iron would be heated up on the fire. Outside, we had quite a small garden and we made use of all the space. There was a vegetable patch in which we grew carrots and potatoes. Opposite was the outside toilet that we had for many years. I remember my mother screaming at my father to, "Get out of that damn toilet!" He'd spend many an hour in there reading his way through the squares of newspaper that hung on a piece of knotted string. Resentfully, he'd depart his little home of solitude and mother would go into the toilet and scrub it clean.

'Mother was a wonderful cook and made the most amazing bread pudding. I have never tasted its equal. She'd leave it to cool on the windowsill, and whenever she wasn't looking, my brother Alf and I would pull off tiny pieces and eat them. Bubble and squeak was a meal we had most days. It was cheap and easy and most of the ingredients were growing in our garden. Lamb or beef was for Sundays, if we could afford it, which was rare, so we often had a vegetable stew or a cottage pie. Mum used to make her own parsnip wine, until one day it exploded during fermentation and stank the house out for days. It made a horrible stain on the wall. She scrubbed at it for weeks afterwards but it never disappeared.'

14

Wartime Duties

Many local people have interesting stories to tell of the wartime period. Even the very young were involved in the war effort, but few had expected the dramatic changes that were to change their lives, for better or worse.

Robert Edgar Proctor was born in Chatham, Kent in February 1927. His family were of Reigate origin and moved back to the borough in 1932, when Robert was five.

'In the spring of 1939, aged twelve, I became a member of the 1st Reigate Boy Scouts, and also of the Reigate St John's Ambulance Brigade Cadets. I attended Reigate Parish School in London Road and lived with my parents and one brother at 31 London Road.

St. Saviours Scouts *(Surrey Records)*, 1910

'It was wartime, and those aged twelve or above were recruited by the ARP to act as messengers to the various posts throughout the borough. I, together with my friend, Sid Best, were allocated to the Red Cross First Aid Post in London Road. We took part in exercises until war broke out, and then our job became much more serious. During those early days, we didn't consider this to be too bad. Our duties were mainly to be at the post from seven in the evening until seven the next morning. We were twelve years old! We slept on stretchers and were accompanied by two ambulance men, who were also in the dugout shelter. The nurses looked after us extremely well. Not too much happened in those early months and it was soon decided that we could stay at home and only turn out if the air raid siren sounded. So it was all quiet until August 1940.

'I was by then thirteen, a regular member of the ARP and issued with a more sophisticated gas mask than those given to civilians. I was also the proud owner of a tin hat marked "ARP". In August 1940, the air raids began properly. The alarm siren would go off whilst I was at school. The teachers and children were evacuated to the air raid shelters. Those for my school were situated in the caves beneath Reigate Castle grounds. I would get my bike from the shed and pedal my way to the First Aid Post. By this stage in the war, it had been decided that ambulance men should be located centrally, so we lost our companions and Sid and I became the only two males on site. Sitting in the post, we could hear the air raid sirens sounding for the general public whenever an attack was imminent, and then again when the all clear was given and the area was considered safe. Workers and children would leave the shelters and return to work or school. However, for we ARP staff, if enemy aircraft were still over the south-east, then the alarm was altered from red to amber and we had to stay at our posts until the green was given. Sometimes, the amber stage could stay all day. Therefore, the education of the young messengers was virtually non-existent. It didn't seem to make much difference anyway as we would be leaving in the next year when we became fourteen.

'During the periods at the post, we were expected to take messages by bike to nurses who were on duty at the air raid shelters and to the ARP Headquarters in Castlefield Road. Luckily, we didn't have too many incidents in Reigate during this stage of the war. One or two people were injured and brought to the Red Cross Post, and Sid and I would have to help them if the doctor was not present. When the main night time bombing of London began, Sid and I were requested to sleep in again, which we did. We didn't like having to take messages out on our bikes during the blackouts, especially if it was a school day the next morning.

'Reaching the age of fourteen, we left school and obtained local apprenticeships. The daylight raids had virtually ceased, so we were rarely called from our workplaces. We both continued our night time duties until we joined the services aged seventeen.'

Percy Brown, a survivor from *HMS Lancastria*, wrote to tell me of how his life was changed by the outbreak of war, but he also gave a short account of his life before he enlisted in the army.

'I was born 1 July 1915. My early recollections begin with my starting school at St Matthew's, which is in Redhill. When I turned six, my family decided to move to Merstham and I enrolled in Merstham Elementary. This was where I was to stay until the leaving age of fourteen. I was very proud to get my first job at the village barber's. I was paid ten shillings per week. I stayed there for just eighteen months. During this time, I learned how to drive and was amazed that the local bobby ignored the fact that I was quite underage to do so.

'It wasn't until the 1930s that I took up the trade that was to sustain me throughout my army career. I got a job as an electrical apprentice in Norbury. This was some distance away so I ended up staying with my grandparents in West Croydon. My rate of pay was four pence an hour, hardly a difference from my days as a barber. Life with my grandparents began to bore me after a couple of years, so I returned to my parents in Merstham. I then had to travel daily to Norbury on the newly inaugurated Green Line Service. This practice continued until 4 April 1933 when the "guvnor" said to me, "Do you drive?" I replied, "Yes. Unofficially." He smiled and asked me to go along with him to get a proper licence. In those times, the Borough of Croydon had its own licensing department in Sydenham Road. All I had to do was fill in a form, pay five shillings, and I came out an official driver! A nice and simple system, better than today's complicated methods.

'I found that by the mid-1930s my wages had improved somewhat, and I decided that I'd had enough of the Green Line Service. So off I went to Pride & Clarke, who were motorcycle dealers. I bought myself a brand new 248cc Panther motorcycle. I soon met my wife to be. We'd been at school together in Merstham, but there'd been no spark between us at that age. On 23 August 1937, we got married at All Saints Church in South Merstham. The church was very crowded. We both came from well-known families of that area. We set up our home in Clyde Road, Addiscombe, not too far from the East Croydon Station.

'When the war broke out, I'd had just over one year of wedded bliss. My life had been proceeding nicely, I'd been employed as an electrician for eight years and had reached the top wage rate of one shilling, ten pence and three farthings an hour. (Nine and a half pence.) My wife became pregnant and Colin was born. Ten days away from his first birthday, we turned on the radio and heard that we were at war with Germany. Practically within minutes the air raid sirens sounded, so we rushed to the garden and the Anderson Shelter. We'd had it dug in earlier for this sort of emergency and we were astounded to discover it full of muddy water! Our next door neighbours had a shelter about ten feet away and theirs was okay. They said we could share theirs, but before we could enter the sirens sounded the all clear. "There will be other times,"' I remember saying to my wife.

'The next day, when I went to work at Norbury, the telephones rang endlessly. People were cancelling the electrical jobs they had previously booked us to do. No-one seemed to know what was happening. I stayed there for another couple of weeks until the staff began to be put off. The "guvnor" said to me, "I don't know what to do about you, Percy." I told him that he wasn't to worry, I had a couple of jobs I could be getting on with. So there I was. I had my cards in my hand and a single hour's pay in lieu of notice.

'I was totally at a loose end and decided to go to Croydon to make enquiries. The depressing result was always the same. "Thank you very much. Please leave your name and address and hopefully we'll be in touch." One organisation did get in touch with me, to my relief. Postal deliveries then came but once a day, in the morning. I opened my mail to see a reply from the Auxiliary Fire Service. I was informed to be at Park Lane, Croydon Fire Station at 9am the next day with enough rations for twenty-four hours. When I got there, I was greeted by an officer for a quick chat, then told to wait. Within an hour, I was told to fall in outside. I fell in with a group of others and stood there whilst a roll-call was performed. When they got to my name I was told that I was wanted upstairs in the office. My mind was filled with curiosity. Surely I wasn't being promoted already? The answer was a resounding no. "We're sorry, Mr Brown, but you're in a reserved occupation as an electrician and therefore we are not allowed to enrol you in the Auxiliary Fire Service."

'So now I was back to my starting point. I had no work and the rent had to be paid. I was lucky enough to get a temporary job at Biggin Hill Aerodrome, but it finished on 31 December 1939. Again, I was given my cards and an hour's pay in lieu of notice. Six days later, on 5 January 1940, I called on my friend Steve Cummings. He lived in the next road and I had worked with him in the past. He informed me that he was going down to the Mitcham Road Barracks in the morning and asked if I wanted to come along. I said, "Yes, but not to join." "No," he said, "that's not the idea." So, we arrived at the barracks about ten in the morning, and when we came out about midday we were soldiers! We'd been told to go away, tell our wives and come back on the ninth of the month, just four days later. We told our families and returned as requested.'

Percy had a varied life throughout his stay in the army. He was in France, Burma and Malaysia, a country that suited him, even the climate. He was on *HMS Lancastria* when it was bombed from above, and swam for nearly an hour and a half before being picked up by a rescue boat. During his time away he was informed that his son, Colin, had died from whooping cough and that his wife was ill. He returned to Redhill for a brief, tearful reunion before he was again shipped out to another destination.

15

How Times Have Changed!

The Walton Comrades Club is a proud institution situated at 7 Franklyn Road, Walton-on-Thames. It has an intriguing story of its own, and a few of its members compiled a short history. Unfortunately, with the exception of the president and vice-president of the club, the members who helped to write the history are no longer living. This chapter, therefore, is dedicated to them. Their names are: J. Howe, J. James, J. Pleasance, T. Tucker, F. Cobbett, J. Poulter, T. Finn, C. Lock and A. Pearson.

In the early months of 1919, a group of mostly ex-servicemen began to hold meetings outside The Crown and The Plough public houses in the village of Walton. The servicemen aimed to start a comrades' club for the area. Fortunately, the Earl Haig Fund had been started just after the First World War, with an interest in launching such organisations. So it was that in the latter months of 1919, "The Club", as it was then simply known, opened above Wood's grocery shop in the High Street of Walton. (This building is now the Nat West Bank.)

The bar consisted of two barrels on top of a couple of planks of wood. The Earl Haig Fund could claim 5 shillings, twenty-five pence, per member. The money collected in this way went towards a purchase of a three-quarter size billiard table and an upright piano. Mr Day from Day Construction in Terrace Road, Walton, is recognised as one of the original barmen. In 1921, the club ceased its operation, though meetings were still held in Walton's Working Men's Club. This became a registered office until the club finally found some more premises.

A plot of land was bought from Gridley Miskins Ltd for £50. The year was 1922 and the money had supposedly been obtained from the sale of the upright piano and billiard table. The land was quite near to the river, much more so than the club's present-day location. Gridley

Miskins operated a timber wharf nearby and believed that their workmen would spend all day in the club, so the purchased site was swapped for today's location. The building of a proper clubhouse could begin. 1923 saw the completion of the timber construction. Basically there was one room – a bar room. The premises were extended in 1926/27, and a concert room was added in addition to a ladies' toilet. Up until that time, the ladies of the club had had to go behind a nearby hedge and they had never been allowed inside the clubroom.

In 1930, an expensive bike shed was added, along with a cellar and underground beer store. Simmonds' Brewery helped the club tremendously through its early years. 1933 saw the government impose an increase in the price of a pint, causing a near riot throughout the country! At the same time, bottled beer was introduced to the club, a fact clearly documented in the AGM reports. Outside, on the lawns which are now a car park, boxing matches were held, and the club also had a strong cricket team. The London Omnibus Company would arrive in double-decker buses to play matches and quench their thirst.

In 1938, Fred Cobbett proposed an idea for a sports day to be held for both men and women. It was carried and proved to be a most successful event. Ted Finn, a valued member, was elected scrutineer at the ballot for officers and committee. In the years leading up to the Second World War, the club steadily grew in size. During the conflict, Vickers (now British Aerospace) took over a local factory that was situated in Tumbling Bay. The components of aircraft were constructed there. The club's concert room was taken over to be used as a workers' canteen. Indeed, Vickers apparently made moves to take over the whole club. This was not resented, however, and the club was paid £1000 for the use of the premises. This money was used for the start of their building fund. During the Second World War, servicemen on leave were given five shillings (25p) spending money from the club funds to make their time off enjoyable.

When the war ended, the club continued to expand. "Tanner Hops" were held on Sunday nights, when you had to pay 6d (a "tanner" or two and a half pence in to-day's money) to go into the concert room to listen to the band. It is recorded that in 1956 the bar takings in the club were £7500. The subs were increased from six shillings (30p) to eight shillings (40p) a year. This could be paid monthly.

The sixties were progressive times for the club, with general improvements being made to the building. The interior was repanelled and a new floor was laid. Courage's helped with a loan. Postcards were soon used for the first time to inform members of the next AGM meetings. Finally, female members were allowed into the clubroom on a Sunday evening to play cards with their husbands or boyfriends. Gordon Willcox proposed in 1963 that the club should allow a fruit machine to raise extra funds. This move was defeated 16 votes for; 52 against. It was then believed that the introduction of such machines would bring the good name of the club into disrepute. However, the decision was reversed the following year and it is without doubt that without those machines the club as it is today would not exist, such a vital part of the club's finances were they.

Various plans were soon drawn up for a new club, and schemes ranging in price were considered. Ladies were granted an associated membership in 1963. Entertainment in the club played a strong part in its history throughout the years. The members formed their own band during the war and they first played together on VE Day, 1945. They were called The Ho-Bos. The present club building was opened in 1974 and built by Rima Construction Ltd. The building is prefabricated and the bar originally ran along the centre of the club with the clubroom on one side and the dance hall on the other. An extension to the cellar and a new bar were built in 1978. Separate rooms for snooker and darts were also created so that there was a large comfortable lounge for the members' use. The dance hall still had a barrel-shaped roof, and it was much criticised as it did nothing for the acoustics of visiting musicians. This was rectified when the last building extension was done, encompassing a television room, a larger downstairs darts and games room and Ladies and Gents toilets. A stage dressing room was also added, and a suspended ceiling to the dance hall area. The club provided accommodation for the Steward and Stewardess in the shape of a bungalow, but this was demolished and a house built in its stead.

Of course, not everybody enjoys the same kind of entertainment, and the club could only hope to please some of the people some of the time. Recognition should go out to all those who got together and practised in an old-fashioned jam session so that they could brighten up the lives of their fellow members. Would the original members of

Walton Comrades Club back in 1919 believe their eyes if they could see it now, seventy-nine years later?

Old Coaching entrance, The Angel Hotel, Guildford *(Surrey Records)*, circa 1920s

16

Milk Money

Ron Gale now lives in Crawley, West Sussex. He shared with me the early years of his working life in Meadvale, Surrey. He first went to work at the age of fifteen.

'I worked for a firm of builders who had an ironmonger's shop. It was situated amongst four shops on the corner of Warren Road and Alma Road, next to what used to be St Mark's Kindergarten School. My family lived in a top-floor flat above these shops. They were owned by a Mr Charlie Hodgson. The shop traded under the name Curringtons, Ironmongers and Builders' Furnishers. Not builders' merchants, but furnishers, an extremely old-fashioned term. At that time the fish and chip shop was on Holmesdale Road, and opposite was Ron Mead's Café and the sweet and tobacco shop owned by Frank Dodds. Jersey Dairies were in Warren Road, and at Mr Alderton's, the stationers in Holmesdale Road, you could buy the original Matchbox toys for one shilling apiece. Not a bad investment considering that some today are now worth quite a bit of money!

'I thoroughly enjoyed these days. They were the times of the great steam trains, an interest of mine. The level crossing gates were operated by hand, by turning a huge, iron wheel. At the last minute, cyclists would rush to beat the gates and either make it through or skid to a halt as the gates lowered with a resounding clang. The gates were fitted with oil lamps. I remember a greengrocer, Kemp I think, whose boxes and crates spilled their wares on the pavement by the gate. It would take forever for the gates to be opened again. If you were on foot, you'd usually end up going over the footbridge, and as you got to the middle the train would pass directly underneath and disperse a large amount of choking steam beneath you. Either bad luck on the pedestrian's part or just good timing by the engine driver? I'll never know. The operator at the gate was a signal man by the name of John

A Guildford Pageant to celebrate of the arrival of steam *(Surrey Records)*, 1957

Johnson. I believe he lived in the cottages at the end of Nutley Lane. I only have one memory of that road. There was a barber's shop at the town end, where you'd pay sixpence for a short back and sides. The barber, Tom Smithers, would endlessly puff away on cigarettes as he cut your hair, and you'd end up being covered in ash!

'I regret the passing of the steam trains. They were magnificent. I can see them now, the sweating fireman and driver lit by the glow from the firebox, white steam turning to vivid crimson as sparks flew from the funnel and the sound of the snorting engines and hissing of the braking mechanisms. Not forgetting the great staff of what was then the old Southern Railway. By necessity, aged twenty-five, I'd taken on second and third jobs, and at this age I found myself with a paper round. I'd rush with my bike from Warren Road to Smith's Bookstall at Reigate Station where I would stuff my round's papers into my bag and hurry to the "down" line to board the 6am train for Betchworth to deliver my wares. Betchworth was a small collection of houses with a cluster of workmen's cottages built around the chalk pits at the foot of the Downs. Most of the houses would be covered in white dust then. My round would end with me cycling up Pebble Hill, a torturous journey for a cyclist! It would take half an hour to climb, but two minutes to free wheel back down! Then I'd cycle back to Reigate and start another job at 8am. They were fun days, although in winter it was tough. I'd invariably get to my day job late. At least the trains always ran on time! Sometimes I'd oversleep and struggle to reach the station by six. I became friends with the train driver and guard, and if I wasn't in sight as he came into the station, he'd give an almighty blast of his whistle! There's nothing more shaming than knowing you're responsible for a noisy, huffing, puffing steam monster complaining about your time-keeping! Once or twice, after I'd been late and the Southern Railway had alerted the whole of Reigate to my shortcomings, a neighbour would grumble about being woken by the noise of the six o' clock train. So if anyone reading this was awoken by that train and didn't know why it made so much noise, well it was for me!

'I believe a failing of my generation these days is to equate most things with "our day". I do believe, though, that our day was better, but then I am biased. Gone are the days of the horse and cart, milk being dispensed from churns straight into your milk jug at the roadside and steam trains are now mostly museum pieces. I'm sure a horse is glad it no longer has to pull a cart, milk is more hygienic and the loss of all that smoke and soot must be better. I wonder, though, how many people were harmed by a horse and cart?

'There were many different types of carts on the roads in our day. Rickett Smith's the coal merchant had a huge, heavy cart loaded with black, tarry sacks full of coal. Its wooden, steel-rimmed wheels had spokes as thick as your arm sprouting out its central wooden hubs. It had a large, square, wooden brake clad in iron, which theoretically was meant to stop the horse from moving. The baker's cart was a little more sophisticated, with delicate little wheels, a comfortable bench for the driver, a curved, wooden hood as a roof and little portholes on the side! The horse itself also looked more elegant, as if it could be a racehorse! Then what about the Oil Man? He was a travelling ironmonger and his cart was painted a dark green with solid rubber tyres. The cart carried this amazing smell of paraffin, soap, wax, polish, leather and candles. There were funnels that hung under the cart next to the horse's nosebag, and you'd be able to load up from these, putting two pennies worth of paraffin in your bottle.

'Lastly, there was the old, two-wheeled milk float. It was more like a chariot, with iron-clad wheels reaching up nearly level with the top of the cart. There was a step on the back on which the driver stood, and I should know because I drove one, with candle lamps on the side and an ornamental, iron centrepiece at the front for the reins to go through and a special pocket for the horse whip. It was my best job ever driving that cart.

'I'd left school aged fourteen and applied for an apprenticeship in the building industry for no other reason than that it was a family tradition. The Second World War had been going on for three years at this time, and apprenticeships were few and far between. I lived in Meadvale, just over the hill south of Reigate. Meadvale was only a tiny village but could boast its own dairy, owned by a Mr Hawkins. Luckily for me, Mr Hawkins needed a delivery man and I needed a job. The only snag was that I was expected to rise at half past four in the morning! Then I had to go to the stable, collect a horse, put on its harness, walk it to the yard a quarter of a mile away, harness it to a dairy float, then load the float with crates of milk. These would consist of half-pint, pint and quart bottles, and they were very carefully stacked to balance.

'My first round consisted of the then newly built Davis Estate. This was three miles away from Meadvale, at South Park. I became an assistant to a milk lady who taught me the round. We'd start at about 5am, which in summer was fine because we'd be finished by midday, unless it was Saturday. This was money day. We'd don leather pouches and collect from each house. Early calls, before seven, were easy: most customers would place the money in paper twists in the milk bottle. But after seven, most people were up, and after chatting, changing money on doorsteps or whatever, we were slowed down considerably and were lucky to be home by three in the afternoon.

'One morning in particular I recall because of a funny incident, though at the time I wasn't laughing. Judy, our horse, was trained to "walk on". She always obliged and was a well-behaved horse, but unfortunately had a hankering for a nice bit of privet hedge. This particular Saturday, I'd just reloaded with fresh milk and had a full cart. I was down the road from Judy and called to her to walk on so that she could level up with me. I was changing some money when I heard an almighty crash and a horse's scream. Judy was lying on her side, the cart was overturned and rivers of milk poured all over the roadside.

Apparently she'd spied a privet hedge and had had to negotiate a small, three-foot bank to get to it, but the cart had overbalanced. Fortunately, Stan Hawkins, owner of the dairy, was having a cup of tea with a customer. He quieted Judy then unharnessed her so she could stand. Stan went back to reload the cart and the customers helped to clear the mess. From then on, Judy decided against eating privet!

'After my first round I would have fifteen minutes for breakfast, usually a cup of tea and a cheese roll, then it was my job to deliver to the cottages inside the grounds of Redhill Hospital. There were only six houses and I would get the milk there on my trade bike. This had a large carrier on the front, a smaller one on back and an advertising metal plate below the crossbar. To get to the hospital, I'd have to ride down Somerset Road. This has a small hill at its eastern end, where it bends to the left and passes a small dew pond known locally as the Chain Pond. At this point you are on the junction of Pendleton Road, where the hospital is situated. One day I was coasting merrily down the hill when my bike suddenly shuddered. Milk smashed into the road and I oversteered the bike. I must have hit the water of the pond at about thirty miles an hour and I ended up being covered in green weed. I never pass that pond now without thinking of that incident and having a little chuckle. An elderly gentleman who lived nearby had hauled me out of the water and moaned about the broken post that I'd hit near the pond and the fact that I'd wasted a lot of milk! No concern for me! For all of this work, I was paid the grand sum of two pounds a week. By the age of fifteen, I'd taken an apprenticeship and then earned fifteen shillings, less four pence National Insurance.

'I also remember the first Morris Mini. Wray Park Garages displayed the first one in Reigate for the princely sum of £575 or thereabouts. Wray Park Garages were situated at the top of Tunnel Road, behind a forecourt of petrol pumps and a row of shops called The Broadway. Tunnel Road used to have two-way traffic running through it. Tesco took over the wine shop at the bottom end, opposite the market pub. The service manager of Wray Park, Mr Bill Kendall, became a close personal friend of mine. We revisited the site many years later from across the roundabout. He thought the place was improved with its clean cut lines of cedar trees and the Margot Fonteyn statue dancing eternally where the Broadway Café once stood. Neither Bill nor I became millionaires, but we did have a zest for living. We always had fun, and yes, things were different in "our day".

17

Legend has it ...

As in all towns and counties, anyone can come across old tales of local folklore and legend. A woman in white, a headless soldier and grey-cowled monks are time-honoured favourites for stories of haunted houses. Indeed, some localities are even named after their spooky cohorts.

My favourite tale of old Surrey has to be this one. There was an old herbalist and witch known as Mother Ludlam. (The name and the spelling of it are different depending upon who tells you the tale!) The local villagers and townspeople would often go to her for help with their various ailments and infirmities. She was a kindly lady and tried to help wherever and whenever she could by mixing herbs and mysterious potions in a large, black cauldron. The Devil was angered by Mother Ludlam for she was mending his work and righting the wrongs that he dealt upon the people. One day he went to her, dressed in a disguise, and asked her to lend him the cauldron. Mother Ludlam was a clever lady and saw past the Devil's disguise, indeed she could see his hoof prints behind him, so she refused him. She turned her back, her only mistake, which gave the Devil the chance to seize the cauldron and make off with it. Mounting her broomstick, Mother Ludlam pursued him. The Devil had put on his Seven League Boots and as he flew from her, he made seven great leaps across the ground. At each footfall, a hill arose. (These seven hills are presently known as the Devil's Jumps.) On the last hill, knowing he couldn't outrun her whilst carrying the heavy cauldron, he set it down and disappeared. (Forming the Devil's Punchbowl.) The last hill is called Kettlebury Hill and is near Hindhead. Mother Ludlam picked up her cauldron and decided that for safety reasons she should take it to a holy place where the Devil could never set foot to steal it again. So, if anyone visits Frensham Church today, a cauldron can be seen.

Many people would argue that this is pure nonsense and has no basis in fact, but this was a story told many years ago when people believed in superstition and magic. In today's society, it is a story that many would scorn, but then it was fully believed to be the truth and so the story is here to stay in the folklore of old Surrey.

We also have the tale of the Surrey Puma. Ask around and most counties will have some mysterious, foreboding beast at large in its countryside. The puma has been spotted by many, but because of the many different descriptions it has been given, it is obviously not the same animal that everyone sees. It has been described as catlike or dog-like, golden in colour, brown in colour, 5ft long and 3ft high, with a dark stripe on its back. Sightings began, reportedly, in Farnham around 1960. Many local animals had been attacked and the injuries -some scratches about five inches long – were attributed to the puma. It wasn't until much later that a renowned zoologist suggested, after studying the supposed tracks, that the prints were actually those of a dog, possibly a bloodhound. Did that explanation suddenly stop the sightings? A resounding no would have to be the answer.

A beast known as The Buckland Shag was said to have haunted an area west of Reigate. It was described as an ape-like animal with a very shaggy coat, and was said to squat upon The Bleeding Stone, a site where a tragic suicide was said to have taken place. (The Bleeding Stone was next to the Shag Brook.) In the early 1800s, a local lord had the stone removed and taken into his own manor grounds. The vicar of Buckland performed an exorcism at the site and the beast was never reported seen again.

Tales of beasts resound around the country, but one ghostly tale has its basis in fact. On Friday, 31 October 1913, Percy Lambert, known as Pearly, took part in a record breaking attempt that ultimately ended his life. He was thirty-two years old and racing was his life. He'd held the speed record in February of that year, doing one hundred miles an hour, but it had been broken by a Frenchman named Jean Chassagne. Percy's car had a 4754cc, four cylinder engine. His sponsor was Lord Shrewsbury. During his attempt, his car came around Member's Hill, a part of the track of the famous Brooklands site, when an eyewitness saw one of his tyres burst. The car swerved, topped the bank and rolled over the cement. During the crash Percy had been thrown from the car and lay upon the track. He was later taken to Weybridge Cottage Hospital but died during the journey there. He was later buried in Brompton Cemetery. It was soon after this tragic accident, that stories were told of a ghostly figure, dressed in goggles and a racing helmet, having been seen upon the spot in which Percy crashed. Strange sounds of roaring engines, squealing brakes and crashing noises are also said to emanate from the site. So the question must be asked. Does Percy Lambert haunt the track that he loved?

Gibbett Hill used to be called Butterwedge until the terrible murder of a sailor that took place on September 24 1786. The sailor was never named, but had befriended three men on a trip to Portsmouth. They had all taken a drink or two at the old Red Lion pub in Thursley before setting off on the final leg of their journey. The sailor was attacked and left to die on the road. The three murderers, Edward Lonegan, James Marshall and Michael Casey, were soon apprehended after the alarm had been raised. They were sentenced to death and left to hang in chains on a gibbet at Hindhead. They hung there for three years, until a terrible storm in the winter of 1789 brought them crashing down.

Newlands Corner in Surrey played a part in a particularly famous false tale just before the Second World War. Agatha Christie was thought to have gone missing, and her car was found there. It was discovered by police, who then combed the woods and forests, searching for the celebrated author. She was eventually found in the north of England.

Ham House in Surrey has reportedly had sightings of a ghost for the past two hundred years. This historic house is open to the public and is supposedly haunted by the ghost of a dog. Many that have reported seeing the spectral canine describe it as being some type of spaniel. This tale was also considered one of the many Surrey hauntings, but could it be true? The recent discovery of the remains of a spaniel dog in the grounds would seem to suggest that it might be.

18

Farncombe Friends

Farncombe is just one stop beyond Guildford, yet from this account it could have been in a completely different county. This is true, rural Surrey in the early years of this century.

"Elsie" was born in the winter of 1911. 'My mum told me that solid rain had lashed down throughout her labour, yet as I was born, the clouds passed and the sun came out for about an hour. She called me her Sunshine Girl. My first few years of life were spent in the tiny village of Binscombe, our house apparently built on what had been the old council tip. The building was small, dark and cramped, lit by smelly gas lamps. It wasn't long before we soon moved to Farncombe. As a young girl, I'd play with my two closest friends, Maisie and Jane. We'd pick wild mushrooms or berries from the fields, and if we felt really daring, go for a paddle in a brook. I say daring because the local boys used to play there, and the first time we went we paddled around holding our skirts until the boys started throwing stones near our feet. Water would splash up our legs and get our underwear wet and my mother would be furious! My family wasn't well off and most of my clothes had been made out of my mother's old, billowing skirts. The local boys also used to hang out by the cricket pitch, I believe it was called Broadwater. In the winter, all children would gather at the lake if it had frozen over. I recall once, during the First World War, the lake was lit by lamps and everyone skated, wrapped up in scarves and hats. At the lakeside, people cooked chestnuts, the smell was delightful.

As a child, I was very much into nature and tried to keep a diary of whatever I saw: thrushes, blackbirds, sparrows, kites, foxes, rabbits, squirrels and moles. There was even a badger sighting once! I'd hear the song of the nightingale but I'd never see it.

'Once, the Canadian soldiers based at Witley put on a performance there and played hockey. When the Canadians left Witley and boarded the train at Farncombe station, the children gathered as the soldiers threw chocolate and candy from the windows. There was a scrabble, I can tell you!

'My school years were at the girls' school in St John's Street. It was extremely strict and the teachers stood for no backchat or messing about. For punishment, we were rapped on the knuckles or had our legs slapped. A man with a horse and two-wheeled trap would deliver the milk and the teacher would ladle it out. I made the mistake once of asking for a second helping and was told off for being greedy. Pocket money was spent on sherbet as far as I can remember. I always thought I'd spend it on something different, but after wandering the shops in Pound Lane, I always ended up buying my favourite sherbet in a twisted paper cone.

'Locally, there was a site where the gypsies would settle for a while each year. I avoided their camps like the plague after my mother's stories of stupid children who wandered into the camps and were never seen again. I know she meant to scare me and she did, but it made me quite biased about the travellers.

'One Saturday afternoon, Maisie and I were out walking. Jane had long since moved to Aldershot in Hampshire. We met up with a boy who lived on Maisie's street. I think he was Peter Martin. He took us to the back of the butcher's shop to show us a pig being slaughtered. He took great delight in my green face. I felt sick to my stomach and ran away. It put me off bacon and ham for a long, long time.

'There was little traffic in those days, hardly any mechanised vehicles. People mostly walked or cycled. The roads were bad, broken stones pressed down as flat as could be, covered with some sort of sand. During winter they'd get wet and muddy or icy and dangerous. In summer they would be dried so hard they were a danger. My family attended church regularly, going three times on a Sunday. I quite liked church and enjoyed the sermons unless it was a sunny day when I wanted to be outside. I remember thinking then that the vicar was a little stiff and boring, his voice a monotonous tone, and he was keeping me from running about under the sun's warming rays.

'I left school aged fourteen and decided not to pursue my education. Money was needed in the house as my father was currently out of work. I got a job at a baker's shop and was allowed to be in the shop front selling the bread and buns. I'd only been there a week when Maisie came to tell me that my mother had died. It had happened whilst she did the laundry in the kitchen, a job she'd hated. Her death devastated me. We held a little funeral with no wake. We couldn't afford it and father refused all offers of help. I knew it was up to me to care for my family and to soldier on. I went back to work the next day, supported by Maisie, who helped me tremendously through that difficult time. As well as keeping a job, I kept house. Cooking, cleaning, laundry, sewing, whilst father did minor repairs or looked after our garden, vegetable plot and chickens. A man would deliver wood for the stove and fire and it was father's job to carry it in, sort it and store it beneath the stairs.

'At that time, I remember thinking that I would never find a husband if I had to care for my father. How wrong I was! I met Henry when I was sixteen and we married when I turned eighteen. Maisie, of course, was my bridesmaid and I made her dress out of a piece of calico that I'd dyed a yellow colour. After my marriage, father got himself a job at Reed's Paper Mill and managed the home on his own until, a couple of years after my mother's death, he met Joan whom he married, and produced my brother, Joe. I had two sons of my own, and in winter took them sledding on High Meadow. This is and has always been a popular hill with the local children, and an excellent choice for sledding. I'd even been down it a few times myself!

'My husband often disappeared at the weekend to shoot pheasants. I remember once, he came home full of pride, carrying his first pheasant. He plopped it on the kitchen counter in front of me and told me he'd like it for his tea. "What do you expect me to do to it?" I asked. He told me to pluck it, gut it and not forget to chop off its head. Memories of the slaughtered pig flooded my mind and I threw the pheasant back at him. "You can do it! You shot the poor thing, you can pluck and gut the damn thing!"

19

Murder Most Foul

Surrey is probably no more famous than any other English county for unpleasant goings-on, but it has had its share of deaths in strange circumstances. These are just two of them:

Emily Jane Popejoy was born in the year 1880. Her family lived in the pleasant village of Bagshot. There wasn't too much employment there and most girls went "in service". Emily was one of these girls. Aged just thirteen, she began work at a home in Reading, Windlesham, and also at the home of a Mr William Rayne, who lived closer to her own home in Bagshot. It wasn't long before the opportunity for a job in London presented itself. A Mrs Camilla Nicholls took Emily on in employment at her house, 14 Pitt Street, Kensington. Mrs Popejoy, Emily's mother, regularly received letters from her daughter stating how much she was enjoying her time at work in the capital city. Just before Christmas 1897, Mrs Popejoy received a letter from Mrs Nicholls stating that her daughter had become ill and that a doctor had diagnosed that Emily had consumption, and had even been consumptive before her employment at Pitt Street had begun.

A concerned relative went to Kensington to collect Emily, hoping that the purer, clean air of the country would have beneficial effects on the poor girl's health. However, when she met up with Emily, she was shocked at the girl's appearance, as were her other relatives when she returned to Bagshot. As well as apparent bad health, the girl's clothes were dirty, torn and stank, her body was covered with bruises and she had a wracking cough. Examining her daughter, Mrs Popejoy discovered that one of Emily's fingers was broken. When asked how it had happened, all Emily could say was that her mistress had done it, that Mrs Nicholls had repeatedly taken to her with a stick and threw her against walls. Other times she'd been starved of food.

Mrs Popejoy, concerned for her daughter's well-being, called her doctor out on Boxing Day. He diagnosed a broken nose, emaciation, a temperature of over a hundred, a weak pulse and bronchial pneumonia. Hearing the alleged tale of abuse, the doctor contacted the police as he believed the girl would not last the night. When the police arrived at the Popejoys' home, Emily was able to tell the policemen how badly she'd been treated by Mrs Nicholls. The next day, as predicted, Emily passed away. She was just seventeen years of age.

The police arrived at Pitt Street to interview Camilla Nicholls. She told them that Emily had arrived at her house in a state of bad health, that the girl had strange habits and ignored orders. Her story was strongly contradicted by the other Pitt Street residents. They reported that there'd been "strange goings-on" at the house, that when Emily had arrived she'd been happy and healthy. One neighbour recounted how Emily would turn up in her back yard, begging for food and water. Two other people stepped forward, having witnessed Mrs Nicholls beating Emily.

News of the case spread throughout the country, causing considerable concern to those families that had daughters in service. Great hostility was directed at Nicholls, whilst sympathy was felt for the Popejoys. At the trial, Mrs Camilla Nicholls was sentenced to seven years for the crime of manslaughter.

John Richardson was killed near Epsom in February 1834. He'd worked as a steward for John Perkins of Bletchingley and his job required him to visit the Epsom Corn Market on a frequent basis, carrying large sums of money. John was a nervous man. The highways and byways were a dangerous place to be for a lone traveller, so he frequently asked for friends or acquaintances to accompany him, along with his two trusty, loaded pistols.

On the morning of 26 February, he was forced to travel alone. Along the way, he observed two suspicious-looking characters hanging around at the roadside. Concerned for his safety, he quickly rode on, but stopped to tell the Tadworth toll keeper about the men. He concluded his business and stopped for a drink. He also took the time to tell his colleagues at the bar about the men. He allegedly was heard to say that if he were to be robbed or killed that night on his way home, then it would be those two characters who had done the deed.

As night fell, it came time for him to journey back to Bletchingley. He followed a road that skirted the Downs then entered a narrow lane that led to Yew Tree Bottom before rising up a hill. As he neared the top of the hill, two figures leapt out from their hiding places amongst the scrub bushes.

John's premonition of his own death must have flashed before his eyes. He always carried one of the loaded pistols ready in his hand, so he took aim and pulled the trigger. Unfortunately, in his panic, he missed his target. Then one of the assailants took out his own pistol and returned fire, fatally wounding John, who fell to the floor.

During this time, there was another traveller out on the road. A man named Mr West. He heard the pistol shots and sought out the sound. He saw two figures running off in the direction of Epsom and gave chase, but he was to lose them in the woods. He returned back to where he'd heard the pistols being fired and came across John Richardson. He was barely alive. West tried to raise John so that he could speak, but before a word was uttered, John died in West's arms. Saddened at being just a moment too late to help this poor man, West picked up John, placed him in his cart and took him to an inn at Banstead, where the police were called.

A reward of £100 was offered in return for information that would lead to the capture of the unknown assailants. Later, John Richardson's employer added a further £100. A magistrate examined the scene of the crime, but there was nothing there that would help the case. No clues had been left behind. All there was, was a vague description of two men who had been seen in the dark. Their descriptions were circulated, but the men were never found.

20

Oxshott and Others

Many Surrey villages have changed almost beyond recognition. Local historian "William", who currently lives in Claygate, had plenty to say about the little hamlet that used to be Oxshott.

'Hundreds of years ago, the place had been called "Occa's Sceat" meaning Occa's strip of land or corner. Oxshott is nestled between Esher and Leatherhead, its borders touching with Claygate and Stoke D'Abernon. Parts of Oxshott and the nearby Claremont Estate were once owned by Queen Victoria and passed down through the family. Many of the roads have new names, named after prominent local residents.

'The main shop in the village had been run by a Mr Manser, who had sold everything under the one roof, and had the local post office in one corner of his premises. The village school was opposite the pond and green. The local doctor lived at Oxshott Lodge, previously called Oakshade House, and his name was Blackwell. This was at the beginning of the twentieth century. The doctor was sometimes helped by the district nurse. By all accounts, a very pleasant, married lady.

'The Bear public house was the preferred drinking hole for most of the locals, though the Victoria Inn, named after the Queen, also did an excellent trade. Up to the year 1818, Oxshott had no school and many people had taught themselves, even though most had difficulty with reading or writing. There was not a large population in Oxshott but there were plenty of children so a school was created in an old barn – the Barn School. This converted barn was also used as a chapel as there was no place of worship in Oxshott either. Those who were church regulars had to travel to the nearest towns for their services. As numbers grew, the need for another school arose and so the Bevendean School, built on the Bevendean estate, was erected.

'There was debate as to when the railway line opened, but most of the residents concurred that the arrival of the trains brought plenty of chances for prosperity in the village. The line ran from Surbiton via Claygate to Oxshott. The main street began on the corner of Oakshade Road in 1895. There was a draper's, confectioner's, tobacconist's, stationer's and a tea room. Then came a hairdresser's, post office, beauty parlour, floor-covering and ceramics, ladies' dresses and an art gallery. It wasn't until 1960 that the first supermarket arrived.'

21

Further Recollections of Old Surrey

The following snippets are short, but they do add details to our picture of old Surrey. They are certainly too interesting to leave out.

'My great-grandparents operated a tollgate on the Ockford road into Godalming. It was one of the main roads through the town, but I don't know exactly what the toll was for or how much it was. My great-great-grandfather was the first policeman in Guildford. His name was Charles Mandeville. He wore a long black coat and a tall top hat called a stove-pipe hat. They were called "pleesmen" then. Charles also became the last keeper of the tollgate.'

'I remember that when the old A3 was built, men from London and Wales came to do the work. As they had no homes in this area, they used to sleep in the underground pipes at night.'

'The Chilworth Gunpowder Factory had a strict policy on not allowing any cigarettes or matches on the premises. Sensible enough, but the people who smoked then, which was a fair few, they had to come up with a scheme. So apparently they used to hide their matches and cigarettes in the hedges in Halfpenny Lane. Whenever they had a break or lunch, they'd nip down to the lane so they could have a crafty smoke.'

'When I got married, I had my wedding cake made covered in a chocolate icing and decorated with chocolate pieces because they couldn't get white icing in those days. We lived in Peasmarsh and my husband was training to be a butcher. We eventually ended up with our own shop, but during his training he was paid the princely sum of £1 and

Guildford Fire Brigade *(Surrey Records)*, circa 1900s

12 shillings. For our own food we'd make up an order and have it delivered from Lipton's. To feed five people with meat and vegetables cost about a pound. From Holdens', in 1938-39, you could get a shilling's worth of bacon pieces that would make a pie to feed five. My husband was demobbed in July 1946 and he was given a docket that would allow him to go to a shop to help set up his home. He could get things like a bed, bed sheets, cutlery, china etc. It was a wonderful idea and helped us out immensely.'

'I was at Croydon Airport in 1927 when Charles Lindberg flew in from Paris in the Spirit of St Louis. There were huge crowds and everybody was cheering. When I saw the plane land, I was hooked. I'm sure that's why I joined the RAF when I was older.'

'My aunt was part of the Women's Voluntary Service during the Second World War. She had a great deal to do and was asked to help rehouse some evacuees, who arrived in trainloads. The children looked so sad, she told me, that she wept aloud. One little girl saw her crying and asked why she was so upset. The question stopped my aunt's tears and she smiled. "You're far from home and family. I have no children and yet a train brings me an instant family. Whatever was Mr Hitler thinking of?"

'Before the First World War, when I was a little girl, I always seemed to remember feeling cold and hungry. Mother said I always woke them during the night, crying about my empty stomach. So one night, before I went to bed, my father crept into next door's garden and stole some eggs from their chickens. Mother boiled me a stolen egg for my supper! Father had been so frightened! There were also pigs and a goat next door, and he thought that they'd make a noise and our neighbours would wake. They didn't. I walked by candlelight up to my room and as I got into bed, blew out the candle. Just as my room went dark, light suddenly flared in from the street outside. The lamplighter had arrived to light the streets. He was a young man on a squeaky bicycle, laden with a front basket. It was a comfort, there in the dark. From then on, my father regularly "borrowed" a few eggs every few nights so that I would have something in my belly and my parents would get a good night's sleep. We lived in Guildford, I can't tell you the street. But if our neighbours are out there, I'm sorry, but I was hungry.'

'I didn't live in what many would call a conventional home. I lived out in the woods past Pyrford. I lived in an old, ramshackle, wooden hut that I'd built myself. I considered myself a decent person, but I did break the law by poaching. A man cannot live off bread alone and the woods could only provide water from the stream, mushrooms and a few berries. Whenever I went out hunting, I'd take my shotgun and take a shot at whatever I came across. There was a manor house close by with a small wood within its grounds that I knew the lord used for pheasant shooting, so I'd often go there. I only once shot a deer because I didn't like the taste of its meat, and the main body was hard for me to sell. Pigeon was my main meal, it tasted a little like chicken. Once, I nearly got caught and was chased through the grounds by the gamekeeper. Scared the hell out of me! Yet that was my lifestyle and that was the way I'd chosen to live. I'm just a boring old man now, living in a two up, two down.'

Mr James Albert Richards was born within the sound of Bow Bells in 1914. However, his family soon moved to Wimbledon, Surrey, as the Germans came over in their air raids and dropped bombs around where he used to live. (Wimbledon is no longer part of Surrey.) He and his brother and sister went to a school in East Ham on Kensington Avenue. The leaving age was fourteen. During his life he had had two wives, women he loved dearly and frequently mentioned. His only other recollections were working at the Midland Bank. Only men worked there. The women stayed at home and reared the children, as they believed it was their duty to do. He never drove a car, but had an old Norton motorbike. He belonged to a motoring club and would frequently attach a side cab and take trips to Land's End in Cornwall. Later, he had bought one of the houses built by the company which built the Kingston bypass.

Mrs Boughton was born in Morden during the Second World War. Her parents had an indoor Anderson Shelter because of the Pylbrook that ran alongside the bottom of the garden and those of their neighbours. 'Garden shelters were always flooding,' she recalls. Her father was not fit for war and so he found himself doing his share of fire watching by standing on the roof of the Lambert and Butler cigarette company on Drury Lane.

When Mrs Boughton was only five years old, she went to The Morden Farm School. 'This is now called Tudor Primary. I remember being taught to hide under my school desk whenever the siren sounded, or to move against the wall.' For morning break, all the children were given half a pint of milk. The bottles had cardboard lids. The classes of those years were overcrowded, some rooms having forty or more children to a class. 'I remember that one teacher had to teach a class in a stockroom cupboard for five years. There was also an awful stench of pig-bins as nearby, in Garth Road, there was a piggery.' Sutton recreation ground was a park for Centurion Tanks. 'My husband, as a boy, would collect pieces of shrapnel from the parks.' Most of the larger houses in the area were requisitioned as billets. 'In Morden town centre, there was a general food office where families were issued with ration books. Everything, it seemed, was in short supply.'

In 1953, the coronation year, they had a street party and took in fancy dress to school. 'We were all given a cup, a plate, and a saucer with the Queen's head on it. Sweets had just come off rationing and lots of the kids had sweet wrappers stuck all over themselves!' Aged fifteen, having unfortunately failed her eleven-plus exams, Mrs Boughton went to work at Fraser Papermill Engineers in Garth Road, Pylbrook Place. It is now Beverley Trading Estate. 'Frasers' had a large bomb drop outside their offices. I think it was because they contributed to the war effort by making the shell covers for our own bombs. It was all pretty scary.'

Caterham is a beautiful part of the Surrey landscape. Driving along on the modern roads, you can look down into the deep, green valley and picture the lifestyle of many years ago. The village nestles in the hillside, protected from the elements, quietly serene and filled with nature at its best. The residents of Caterham go along at their own pace and most are, and always have been, extremely happy to be there.

Mr Worsfold was born in 1930 at 108 Farningham Road, Caterham. His family moved to 8 Commonwealth Road, Caterham when he was seven years of age. 'The Caterham Railway was known to us all at that time as "Paddy's Heaven" because of all the Irishmen working there. There was no gas or electricity and lighting was obtained by using paraffin lamps. At home, we had accumulators to run the wireless. I remember that our favourite programmes to listen to were *The Archers, Dick Barton, Family Favourites* and *In Town Tonight* among others.

'A family from Caterham on the Hill moved into 10 Commonwealth Road. Their names were Mr and Mrs Bishop. I went to the board school with their daughter, Kathleen, who was also seven years of age. If we wanted to go shopping, we'd go to Caterham Valley. There was a Co-op, Home and Colonial World Stores, International Stores and Cullens, which have now all gone. We still have a Woolworth's. There are two pubs called Old Surrey Hounds and The Fountain. Previously, there were The Greyhound and The Valley Hotel. The local cinema was called the Capital.

'Aged eleven, Kathleen and I went to the Central School at Wasp Lodge, Caterham. We left at age fourteen. I went to the Co-op as a trainee, and Kathleen went to Beasley Lampshades in Stafford Road to work in the shop, then to Woolworth's. We courted and got engaged, then married in 1954.'

The lobby of the Angel Hotel, Guildford *(Surrey Records)*, circa 1920s

Also of interest:

Best Tea Shop Walks in Surrey & Sussex

Best Tea Shop Walks in The Chilterns

Best Tea Shop Walks in Hampshire

Best Tea Shop Walks in Suffolk

(Note: Many more areas are covered in our 'Best Tea Shop Walks' series; each book is £6.95)

By-Way Biking in The Chilterns *(£6.95)*

Best Pub Walks in & around Central London *(£6.95)*

Best Pub Walks in Essex *(£6.95)*

Dogs' London: The City's Best Walks for Dogs and their Owners *(£6.95)*

London Bus-Top Tourist *(£6.95)*

Railway Rambles: London & The South-East *(£4.95)*

Walks in Mysterious Hampshire ***(£6.95)***

A Year of Walks: Sussex ***(£6.95)***

West Sussex Church Walks ***(£7.95)***

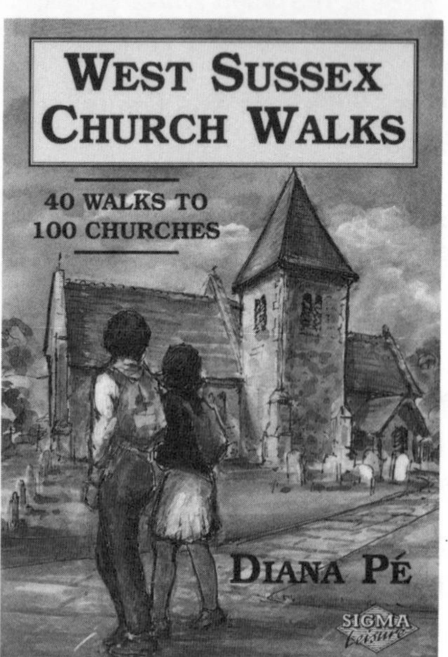

All of our books are available through your local bookseller. In case of difficulty, or for a free catalogue, please contact:

SIGMA LEISURE, 1 SOUTH OAK LANE, WILMSLOW, CHESHIRE SK9 6AR.

Phone: 01625-531035;
Fax: 01625-536800.
E-mail:
sigma.press@zetnet.co.uk .

Web site:
http//www.sigmapress.co.uk

VISA and MASTERCARD welcome. Please add £2 p&p to all orders.